The Light Behind God

What Religion Can Learn

From Near Death Experiences

Rene Jorgensen

To all the innocent who have suffered

at the hands of man's angry God.

Contents

Acknowledgments   9

Introduction   11

Chapter 1   A Source of Religion   17

Chapter 2   No Other Source than God   31

Chapter 3   The Nature of the Light   49

Chapter 4   Death and Resurrection   61

Chapter 5   The Light is Not Angry   73

Chapter 6   Adam's Alibi   93

Chapter 7   Hell as a Gift   111

Chapter 8   God Within   133

Chapter 9   Heaven's Gate   153

Resources   181

Acknowledgements

I wish to thank the people who have contributed to my research with their near death experience and profound insights of heaven. I thank you all for sharing your personal testimonies, which now serve as much needed voices to bring light into our present day and age.

I also want to thank the International Association for Near Death Studies for their brave investigation into the phenomenon of near death experiences and the mystery of what lies beyond death. And a special thanks to Charles Swedrock for taking the time to edit the first edition of this book.

Rene Jorgensen

June 2011

Introduction

This book is based on an in-depth investigation of the parallels between near death experiences and religion. Since religion is founded on the belief in life after death, near death experiences that happen during clinical death have an obvious connection to this foundation.

For various reasons, most research of near death experiences has clearly been separated from the category of religion. However, opposite this separation, the aim of the research project behind this book has been to try to shed light on the similarities and possible parallels to religion.

I have been undertaking this research project for over three years and it is founded on an in-depth questionnaire of 16 people who have had a near death experience. Each person has filled out an NDE Scale (Dr. Bruce Greyson's NDE Scale) to verify and evaluate their experience.

11 of the 16 cases were close to physical death. Two cases happened during severe illness and another two cases during deep spiritual inspiration. One case happened during a drug induced state that brought the person close to death.

With a medium score of 16 for a near death experience, the cases in my study have an average score of 21, which means that they range from deep to very deep near death experiences.

I have focused my research on deep near death experiences because NDE research suggests that the deeper the experience the more we can learn about the nature of the experience. My reason for analyzing 16 different near death experiences is to arrive at a more objective interpretation of the contents of the experience that relates to religion.

My research project consisted of a 15 page questionnaire and almost 20 hours of interviews and testimonies from near death experiencers. The conclusions of the research are based on statistical analysis of the questionnaire and the interviews have been used as testimonies throughout the book to speak directly to the reader. The questionnaire was based on a multiple choice questionnaire with different random choices and statements that each participant was asked to either agree with, disagree with or state that they were not sure about the answer.

The conclusions of the research have then been made based on the level of agreement among the participants, which means that the conclusions are relating to general consensus. I have calculated the level of consensus in percentage with a margin of error of 6 percent and plus or minus 1 percent in rounding the numbers up or down.

This has been done so that the conclusions of the research are based, not on one subjective interpretation but instead on the level of agreement in the interpretation between the 16 participants.

I have done this in order to locate a more objective interpretation of the near death experience. Each near death experience has a certain level of personal content, which results in a subjective interpretation of the experience. But by looking for common elements and a universal agreement within the experience, I believe that we can get closer to a more truthful interpretation of the near death experience.

My intention behind this is to share the profound messages from the Light in the near death experience, which I truly believe holds a very important message for organized religion and especially dogmatic interpretation thereof. Part of the research in the book has also been published under the title *Behind 90 Minutes in Heaven,* as a response to Don Piper's misuse of his near death experience to support religious fundamentalism.

In over 30 years of research of near death experiences there is absolutely no objective evidence to support religious fundamentalism, and as you will find with this book, I feel strongly about making this case. The research of near death experiences firmly concludes that there is no such thing as an angry God and that we should all truly love our neighbor. While I know this conclusion will upset some religious people, I have also attempted to provide the reasons behind this conclusion based on objective research. I truly hope that the research behind this book will serve as a reasonable dialogue with religion and help some believers to get closer to God.

I should also say that while I have attempted to answer new and deeper questions through my in-depth questionnaire, overall I am still relying on generally accepted research of near death experiences. I do so because I am well aware that 16 cases of near death experiences, while in-depth, still this is a small sample. The general research of near death experiences that I am relying on and the conclusions hereof, has been collected during more than 30 years and through many studies involving thousands of cases of near death experiences.

Last I just want to let my reader know that this book has been self-published in its current edition. I hope that you will be able to see beyond possible imperfections and value the research and insights that would otherwise not have been available to you.

Chapter One:

A Source of Religion

In order to draw parallels between the Near Death Experience and religion, I will begin with a short out-line of what a Near Death Experience (NDE) is. An NDE is an extraordinary otherworldly experience that in the infinite nature of its powerful revelation is beyond human comprehension.

Here in this world and with the tools we have available, we typically define the NDE as a profound psychological and spiritual experience that occurs during intense situations such as clinical death or trauma. Similar experiences can be traced back to pre-historic time, but the term "Near Death Experience" was first coined in 1975 when Dr. Raymond Moody published the book *Life After Life*. Moody's interest had been awoken by people who were close to physical death but soon after the term was coined it became clear that similar experiences happen under very different circumstances.

Illness, intense fear, giving birth, deep prayer, meditation, vision quests and drug induced states, are all other causes that produce very similar or identical experiences. The fact that very different events can produce the same experience suggests that the phenomenon of the NDE points to a state or dimension that has many different doors. Therefore, the NDE as an experience is defined by universal core features.

These core elements include a sense of being in an otherworldly place, which often begins with an Out-of-Body experience where the person is able to see her-or himself from outside the body. Some people will describe rapid movement through a tunnel, while others will describe being a point of awareness having tunnel vision.

Then, many people will experience an overwhelmingly intense emotional experience of profound love, peace and joy, which most people describe coming from a source of a brilliant clear light that is most commonly referred to as "the Light." This light is described as a brilliant white light of unearthly beauty, which is intensely bright and radiant without hurting the eyes.

Dannion Brinkley explains in *Saved by the Light* that:

Ahead the light became brighter and brighter until it overtook the darkness and left me standing in a paradise of brilliant light. This was the brightest light I had ever seen, but in spite of that, it didn't hurt my eyes in the least. Unlike the pain one might feel when walking into sunlight from a dark room, this light was soothing to my eyes.

The meeting with this light is then followed in some experiences by a positive and/or negative life-review, where people see positive or negative episodes from their life flash by before their eyes. The positive life-reviews are part of so-called pleasant experiences or "heaven-like experiences" and these share strong parallels to the religious understanding of heaven. Opposite these negative experiences within the NDE, which can range from painful life-reviews to so-called "hell-like experiences" or "hellish-experiences," share many similarities with the religious concept of hell.

Some people will be guided through their life-review by a relative, religious figure or a being of light, while others will experience it alone in a formless state. Many people also testify that the Light, or this other dimension, gives them a sense of total and absolute knowledge about everything that there is to know about the entire universe.

At the last stage of the experience, some people will be told to return to their body while others will simply return automatically.

Upon returning to this world again most people will say that their experience is indescribable and unlike anything that they have ever experienced in this world. While many people will feel confused and overwhelmed months or sometimes even years after the experience, it is the sheer power of this otherworldly experience that gives people a very strong conviction that what they experienced is real.

Therefore, the NDE is described as more than real, or 'hyper-real.' Even though Near Death Experiencers (NDErs), people who have NDEs, generally prefer seeing themselves as spiritual and not religious, most of them will still use the term "God" about their experience. In their testimonies, the Light or Truth, in their experience is often described as the true nature of being or the ground of being. NDErs experience the ultimate state of being as coming before their maker, God, in a very broad sense.

For all of these reasons, it is easy to understand that many NDErs and NDE researchers are convinced of a link between the NDE and religion. Raymond Moody, the father of the NDE, was the first to suggest that most of the world's great religions were either started by or had gained their inspiration from individuals who have had an NDE.

If we take a look at religion with these perspectives in mind, it is easy to find many parallels between religion and the NDE. In the Christian religious tradition, Genesis begins with God's creation of the world through: "Let there be light." Later we are told that; "God is love" and that "God is light," and also in John we find this long reference to light:

In him was life, and the life was the light of men. And the light shines in the darkness; and the darkness grasped it not. There was a man, one sent from God, whose name was John. This man came as a witness, to bear witness concerning the light, that all might believe through him. He was not himself the light, but was to bear *witness to the light. It was the true light that enlightens every man who comes into the world.*

In the Bible we also find meetings between God and man as what people describe in the NDE. In Exodus, God appears to Moses in the form of a burning bush, and when Moses asks about God's name or who he is, "God said to Moses: I AM WHO AM." In the footnote of verse 14 in the 1609 Douay Version of the Old Testament, we are told:

I am who am. That is, I am being itself, eternal, self-existent, independent, infinite; without beginning, end, or change; and the source of all other beings.

This description of who God is, or what the nature of God is, shares many similarities with the essence of the experience that NDErs give testimony to. Also if we take a look at the revelations or religious experiences that have inspired religion, we will find that there are many parallels to the NDE.

After the Exodus where the people of Israel are led out of Egypt, Moses goes back up on Mount Sinai and spends forty days and forty nights in the presence of God. Here Moses describes the sight of God as a "burning fire," and it is upon this meeting that Moses receives the law of God in the form of the Ten Commandments.

In the New Testament we also find that Jesus spends forty days and forty nights in the desert where he is tempted by the devil. This time spent in the desert comes just before Jesus goes to Galilee to begin his preaching, and Luke tells us that Jesus returned from the desert "in the power of the Spirit."

From this sequence of events it would clearly seem that Jesus had a revelation or religious experience during his forty days and nights in the desert, and that this was part of the inspiration to begin his ministry.

We find this same ritual of fasting in isolation to be closer to God, or the Great Spirit, in aboriginal religion.

In Native American tradition this fasting in isolation is called Vision Quest and it is used as a death and rebirth ritual to restore spiritual power and provide guidance. We also find evidence of near death experiences among the Native Americans such as the vision of Tenskwatawa.

After falling sick Tenskwatawa explains: "I died and went to the World Above, and saw it. I have come back cleansed. I am as we were in the Beginning! In me is a shining power!"

In the religion of Islam we find a similar path to God, where the Prophet Muhammad retired to meditate in the solitude of the cave Hira in Mount *Jabal Al-Nur*, the Mountain of Light. In the Islamic tradition it is said that it was during one of his meditations in the cave that Muhammad received a call from God, or Allah, to go forth and preach.

This was during the month of Ramadan and for this reason still today Muslims are fasting during this month. In this cave the Quran was revealed to Muhammad and he later declared that the same heavenly message that Moses had received, had also come to him as the prophet of Allah.

In the Quran, Surah 17, we find the testimony of Muhammad's so-called "Night Journey" into the seven heavens and it is explained that he went on this journey in the spirit as he left his body behind. Surah 44 tells us that the enlightened scripture of the Quran was sent "down in a blessed night," and Surah 53 explains that this "was divine inspiration" dictated by the most powerful from the highest height "where the eternal Paradise is located."

In this divine place Muhammad was "overwhelmed" and he saw "the great signs" of his Lord, even though his eyes "did not waver, nor go blind." Similar to what people experience in their NDE, here in the Quran we clearly have the meeting with God, or Allah, in paradise and an overwhelming sight of the Lord, which was bright enough to otherwise make someone blind.

Also if we look at the Eastern religion of Buddhism we find that meditation plays a central part and that light is a key part of enlightenment. The Buddha became enlightened after meditating for forty-nine days under a Bodhi Tree and then contemplating this experience for seven days after. It is said that all the 84,000 teachings of the Buddha can be condensed into one line – *recognize your essence* – and if we go back to God's nature as *being* itself in the Old Testament, the parallel is very similar.

Also if we look at the Tibetan tradition of Buddhism we find that light is a central part of enlightenment. Here the true nature of reality, the ground of being, is called "Clear Light" nature, which can be reached through meditation during our life or through enlightenment when we die.

In the *Tibetan Book of the Dead*, which is a guide to enlightenment at death, this clear light is described as: "The subtlest light that illuminates the profoundest reality of the universe...It is an inconceivable light, beyond the duality of bright and dark, a light of self-luminosity of all things."

This description of the clear light in Buddhism as the ultimate nature of reality is very similar to the light that people describe in the NDE.

Going back to the death and rebirth rituals found in aboriginal cultures, we also find the Eleusinian Mysteries in ancient Greek culture. These secret ceremonies are believed to date back to around 1600 BC and involved visions of the afterlife and sacrifices to the Greek gods. The mysteries included the mythology of Demeter and her daughter Persephone, who was taken to the underworld kingdom by Hades, the God of the Underworld.

The immortality of the soul was standard in Greek thinking and one can be pretty confident in suggesting that the near death experience was also part of Greek thinking, as the great philosopher Plato gives an almost certain account of an NDE in his work *The Republic*.

Here we find a soldier, Er the son of Armenius, who after dying in battle returns to life after being dead for twelve days. He comes back and tells that he has seen "the other world" when his soul left the body and went on "a journey" to a "mysterious place."

In this place he also encounters a light as he explains that he came to a place where he "could see from above a line of light, straight as a column, extending right through the whole heaven and through the earth, in color resembling the rainbow, only brighter and purer."

Er calls this light the "belt of heaven" that holds together the "circle of the universe," and he talks about ascending into the heavens above with "exceeding joy." All of these elements are very similar, if not identical, to what people experience in the near death experience, and we also find in Plato's *Phaedo* that the true meaning of life is first revealed to us when we die.

In the same way that people who have NDEs testify, Plato tells us that the true meaning of life is revealed after death when we enter the "true heaven" above and are able to see life on earth in its "true light."

In Egypt we can still see the Great Pyramids that where built to help the Pharos ascend into their celestial homes after death. For the Egyptians the structure of the cosmos consisted of three parts: Sky, Earth and Underworld, and while the sky was an endless cosmic sea, the earth existed within a bubble.

Central to Egyptian religion we find the *Egyptian Book of the Dead*, which like the *Tibetan Book of the Dead* is a guide to the afterlife. As part of these books we find in the *Book of Gates* references to light, where the final hour of the night brings the deceased through a mysterious gate to the meeting with the gods who "carry the blazing light."

A central theme for the Egyptians was the Egyptian god Ra, the Egyptian sun god. Through Ra, symbolized by the sun, light played a key role in the realm of the dead as a life-giving force. So, as with people who have NDEs we find a clear parallel to the emphasis on light as a key element in Egyptian afterlife.

Also in one of the oldest writings in human civilization, written on clay tablets, we find in ancient Mesopotamian religion the *Epic of Gilgamesh*. Here King Gilgamesh goes in search of eternal life, and after traveling through a dark tunnel through the twin mountain of Mashu, he reaches a light at the end of the tunnel and finds himself in a miraculous garden of jewels.

This garden is on the heavenly side of the border between the divine and human world, and it shares many parallels with the Garden of Eden in Genesis of the Old Testament. In the *Epic of Gilgamesh*, we also find a story of the Flood almost identical to the Great Flood of the Bible, and this flood story is believed to be one of the early sources for the flood in the Bible.

In general we can say about religion that the concept of heaven and hell is universal, since it is found in practically all religions. Also we find the reference to light as a key element in most religious cultures, and it would thus be reasonable to ask where these universal concepts have arrived from.

Here it would be logical to conclude that the universal arrival of the same elements must have come from the same source. Based on the fact that most religions have been founded on revelations or religious experiences, it would therefore also seem reasonable to suggest that the NDE could be such a source of inspiration.

Another NDE researcher, Dr. Peter Fenwick, has suggested that while many people believe that the NDE provides us with glimpses and proof of heaven or hell it could also just as reasonably be assumed that it is the NDE itself, which has shaped our very ideas of heaven and hell.

Fenwick explains that,

Every culture has an idea of Heaven and an idea of Hell. They vary according to the culture but the question is: where did these ideas arrive from? The near death experience is something that people will have had all throughout the ages, so it is logical to assume that this [the

NDE] is something that would be understood as intensely religious.

There is also little doubt that all religions aim to create order out of chaos, and in the same way we find a universal law in the NDE that clearly has this purpose. The life-review, which can be very painful in the review of harmful actions, has been called the "ultimate teaching tool" and is seen by many NDErs as an indisputable law of the universe.

From this law of the universe behind the life-review most NDErs will conclude the indisputable truth of the Golden Rule that we find in all religions. So, not only through parallels in the contents of light, heaven and hell but also through the motivation to love our neighbor, we find common ground between religion and the near death experience.

Some fundamentalists in the Christian tradition will use one line in the Bible, which says that Satan masquerades as an angel of light, to reject the NDE in the effort of trying to uphold their patent on God. However, here it should be remembered that the Bible also says that there is no darkness in light and that Jesus told us exactly how to recognize false prophets: "By their fruits you shall know them."

This is where the universal conclusion of the Golden Rule in the NDE comes in. As an aftereffect of the NDE, one of the most powerful testimonies of the reality of the NDE is that most people who have NDEs report significant life-changes after their experience. People change their job, place of living or their partner, but most radical are the changes in behavior.

Many studies have found that by far the majority, 80 – 90 percent of NDErs, report radical changes in their attitude towards other people, such as becoming more loving, compassionate, joyful, tolerant, forgiving, and finding an increase in their desire to help others.

The research also finds that the deeper the NDE and the more intense experience of the Light, the greater the transformation of the individual. Therefore, these positive life-changes are seen as an authentic response to the nature of the Light, because people are convinced these qualities are the true nature of reality.

Satan on the other hand does not produce these positive fruits of the Light: love, compassion, joy, tolerance, forgiveness and wanting to help others. These authentic responses to the Light could only come from a source that has these qualities, and thus, as Jesus says the goodness of the fruit gives testimony of the source of the fruit.

As such, listening to the authentic message from the Light in the NDE – *the Light behind God* – makes real sense to any person who believes in God.

Chapter Two:

No Other Source than God

In chapter one, I began by explaining that identical experiences to Near Death Experiences (NDEs) can happen under very different circumstances. We saw that religious experiences or rituals together with revelation and meditation or prayer can produce very similar experiences.

However, in our modern world ruled by science it is mostly the cases of NDEs that involve clinical death that attracts the most attention. This is understandable since we are naturally curious about what death holds for us, and no other event or phenomenon brings us closer to death than these NDEs where people are clinically dead.

Some people will argue that clinical death is not dead enough or that people have not been dead for real. But a person being clinically dead is not a small thing. When a person is clinically dead it means that the person has cardiac arrest with no breathing, no pulse, no brainstem reflexes and pupils that are dilated and fixed.

These are the internationally recognized signs of death, and a person experiencing these conditions is considered dead both from a medical and scientific point of view.

While this state of clinical death is reversible for a short amount of time, a person experiencing this state is still considered dead.

So, according to our present knowledge people who have been brought back from clinical death have in effect not been *near* to death but have actually been dead. This means that the NDE is one of the most reliable accounts about life after death since these people have actually been dead or at least as close as we can get.

Some of the most challenging cases to our present scientific paradigm are the cases of NDEs where the brain activity has been monitored during cardiac arrest. The most famous case is the case of Pam Reynolds, who underwent a complicated brain surgery in 1991, where she was clinically dead for 55 minutes during which time she had no brain wave activity.

She had an uninterrupted out-of-body and near-death experience extending from before this time into the almost one hour she was clinically dead, and she reported events during the time her brain was inactive. Also with her eyes taped shut and her hears filled with earplugs that had a clicking sound, Reynolds should not have been able to observe anything, but was able to see and hear everything happening in the operating room. After the experience she was able to describe both the instruments used and to repeat the conversations between the doctor and the nurse during the operation.

All of her observations were objectively confirmed and there have been many other similar cases and studies of what is called "veridical perception" in NDEs, where people see things while outside the body that are later objectively confirmed.

Also researcher Dr. Kenneth Ring did a study of 31 blind people that had had an NDE. To his surprise 80 percent said that they were able to see while having their NDE, and what makes his study really interesting is that 14 of these blind people had been blind from birth.

So, the skeptics are left with some tough questions that challenge their creativity: How can people have experience with clear consciousness when their brain is inactive? And how can people who are blind and have never been able to see, suddenly see during their NDE?

Convincing answers to these questions are most likely to be found beyond the frontier of new science and will probably not be answered before we know more about consciousness: what it is and where it is produced.

For now let's just say that the judge is still out for the materialists that demand solid proof. However, while the judge is out and present scientific knowledge can only account for 4 percent of our universe as physical matter, it is not unreasonable for those of us with faith to assume that there is something more out there beyond our limited spectrum of reality.

Strongly suggesting that we do not live in a confined 4 percent universe, the NDE is an anomaly that points towards the 96 percent of our unknown universe. While skeptical theories within a 4 percent universe paradigm have tried to explain away the NDE, no accepted theory to date is able to explain all elements of the NDE. The NDE remains a challenge for the future and while some prefer to live in a flat world till then, others are able to look towards the future through the research of NDEs.

As we saw in the last chapter, in all religions we find a source of revelation behind the written words and as a revelation of an otherworldly source there is no other experience or phenomenon as powerful as the NDE.

People who have NDEs are themselves persuaded that their experience represents something truly authentic and real beyond any shadow of doubt. From their point of view, or rather with this insight, it is often hard for these people to understand why the world around them tends not to believe what they bring back.

I am confounded by why people wonder if it's real. If I were to take an airplane ride and go to another city and then come back, and I said: "I was just visiting so-and-so place," no one would ask: "Are you sure? Are you sure you went?" And yet, this was much more real than that.

What Connie expresses here is typical for most people who have an NDE. The place that they have been to on the other side is as real as anything in this world, and in fact, more real than that; as Melanie describes it, "Beyond anything that can be experienced in this world."

This sense that the experience is more real than real, was one of the first things that I focused on in my study. I believe this point to be one of the most important and convincing pieces of evidence since these experiences are testifying about another dimension that is of a higher or bigger reality outside our limited spectrum of reality.

In my questionnaire, I asked each Near Death Experiencer (NDEr) if they agreed or disagreed with the following statement: "The power of my experience, which is beyond anything that I have ever experienced on earth, made me absolutely sure that my experience was real."

More than nine out of ten, 93 percent, said that they either strongly agreed or agreed with the statement, and this consensus clearly suggests that we are dealing with a very different and unusual experience.

As the statement points out, it is the force of the experience that convinces the NDEr beyond any doubt that their experience is real, because the sheer power of the otherworldly dimension that they experience is so overwhelming that it does not leave room for any doubt.

With this insight I wanted to get closer to understanding the power of the experience, so I asked each NDEr to compare the sensation in their NDE to the sensation of experience here in this dimension on earth.

Here 81 percent said that the sensation was stronger than here on earth, with 25 percent saying 50 – 100 times stronger than in this dimension, and 56 percent saying a thousand times stronger or beyond description. In the category of a thousand times stronger or beyond, I got statements such as; "beyond my ability to describe," or it "cannot be measured," and Priscilla gave this very good explanation that it's,

Something that cannot be put into words. Part of the reason for this is that the experience of leaving this dimension and entering another is a very powerful sensation.

As Priscilla explains; it is the event itself of leaving this world and entering another dimension in the Out-of-Body state that induces such a powerful sensation that cannot be put into words. And while this experience cannot be described exactly in human language, the sheer power of it still speaks so loud that there is no room for doubt in the mind of the experiencer.

To make a parallel to experience in this dimension, we would have to imagine a state of heightened awareness, e.g. a situation where we almost had an accident. In the moments just before the accident we will experience an extreme sense of heightened awareness and sharpened focus to help us avert the accident. Most of us will have no doubt about the reality of this situation, in fact, some of us may say this moment is more real and even note upon the sense of timelessness.

This is the sort of sharpened awareness and intensity of sensation that NDErs experience in their NDE, only it is much more powerful than anything in this dimension and this sheer power of the experience is the convincing factor.

It is also this convincing power that makes the NDE different from a dream or a hallucination. Given that a dream or hallucination is often used to explain away the NDE, I asked the NDErs to compare their experience to a dream or hallucination. To the statement, "What I experienced could have been a dream or hallucination," 86 percent said that they either strongly disagreed or disagreed.

When I turned the question around and asked the NDErs about the following statement: "What I experienced was very different from a dream or hallucination," I found that 93 percent said that they agreed with 80 percent saying that they strongly agreed.

From this result, it is very clear to the experiencer that the experience has a distinctive quality, which is unlike anything else in this dimension, and that the experience is not like any dream or hallucination.

One NDEr puts it like this:

I am convinced that my experience is real. Everyone has had a vivid dream and anyone who is sane can tell the difference between a vivid dream and an experience. Having the experience itself is the convincing factor and that cannot be expressed in words.

We all know the difference between a dream and reality, maybe not while in the dream but surely after the dream is over and we return to this reality again. It is the same for any sane person having a hallucination. After the hallucination is over, most people will know what is real and what is not. This is the same for people who have NDEs; after coming back NDErs are also able to clearly distinguish their experience from a dream or hallucination.

To elaborate on this point and build upon the last insight of the sense of a stronger reality, it is not uncommon to have NDErs suggest that this world is ultimately a dream. Connie tells us that, "It is the most real experience I've ever had. It is more real than waking up from a dream here on earth."

If we here think about the feeling of waking up from a dream and the exact moment our mind refocuses to distinguish the dream from reality. That is how the NDE is experienced, only this world is the dream and the other dimension is reality, and this is what is meant by the otherworldly and higher-dimensional nature of the NDE.

There is also another distinguishing factor that separates the NDE from dreams and hallucinations, and that is the fact that most people who have NDEs remember the experience clearly many years after. Where dreams and hallucinations are often forgotten after some time, the memory of the NDE stays clear in the mind of the NDEr many years after.

Michael confirms this here:

My experience was real to me. It was real to me because eight years later, I still see what I can consciously remember with absolute clarity – the Light, the people, the peace. Clinically dead at the time, I should have no memory at all, but I do – stronger than any waking or dreaming moment.

When you add the power and intensity of the NDE to the fact that people remember their experience with great clarity many years after, then you have the argument why we should listen to these testimonies. They speak louder than any other phenomenon known to man, or we could say that God speaks louder to us through these experiences, and this is a good reason to listen.

I also asked the NDErs to rate "how real" their experience was to them from 10 to 1000 percent. Here two thirds said more than 100 percent with 53 percent answering "1000%" real. This was of course a trick question to highlight the otherworldly sense of reality as in our normal understanding nothing can be more than 100 percent. However, Russ was cleaver to point out something important, "How can anyone quantify a particular number without anything to compare it to?"

This is really a central point; that there is nothing else to compare the NDE to in this dimension and this is the reason that a reference to God is often made within this experience. There is simply no other experience or reference point here in this world that compares to what is experienced in the NDE, and therefore, the NDEr is forced to use the realm of God to explain what they have experienced.

When asked: "What would you describe the core or essence of your experience as," my study found that 53 percent checked the box with "pure being," and 60 percent said yes to "essence of existence." Moving further into trying to put a name on this core or essence, the consensus became even greater with 73 percent agreeing to call it "the Light." The greatest consensus was found through the religious word "God," where 80 percent agreed to call the core of their experience – the experience of "God."

Usually people who have NDEs prefer to call themselves "spiritual" rather than "religious," since organized religion will often seem too confined or limited for what they have experienced. However, while experiencers will sometimes object to using the word "God" it is clear that if we look behind the disagreements of how to interpret God, what this name points towards has very clearly something to do with what people experience in their NDE.

If you want to call the light God. I have no trouble calling it God. To me it was God and it was for a long time. Now, I think of it as a greater consciousness that we are all part of or something like that. But that can be called God too, so I don't have any difficulty calling it God.

Here David agrees to call the light God but he clearly also tries to open up the concept, which is something that we often find with people who have NDEs. Generally in NDE research, NDErs tend to use the term a "being of light" and while they will use God to describe this form of being, it is to be understood as God in a very broad sense. Rather than an experience of God that fits a particular religion, NDErs will have an experience of God in a sense that is spiritually neutral and bigger than any human conceptual understanding.

It is only natural to human nature to use the tools available to us, especially if our ability to comprehend is pushed to the limit as in the NDE, and therefore, many people will use their religious background to makes sense of the experience. Few NDErs or certain people will go so far as taking the NDE beyond a level of certainty and use the experience as evidence of a specific religious tradition or its dogma.

Still the fact remains that most NDErs and by far the majority of the research holds firm that 'God' is spiritually neutral and to be understood very broadly. In remembering that our language and comprehension is limited, what these people experience is something beyond a conventional understanding of God – as something *behind* God.

Next to the 80 percent agreeing to call what they experienced "God," I also found that two thirds of the NDErs in my study would agree to call this "the Light of God." I should here mention that most studies will use the term "the Light" because the category of God and religion has been left out of many studies. I was, however, as were 80 percent of the NDErs in my study, not against using the term "God."

What I knew when I came back was that I know that light was of God. It was of or from God. I didn't think the light itself was necessarily God, although it could be, I don't know. But I know that that light is a part of God...or a part of what God emits.

As this testimony from Jayne is explaining; the light in the NDE is *of* God. This is also a general conclusion in research of NDEs, and as mentioned, some religious people have refused to accept this apparent parallel by using one line in the Bible about false prophets, where they are told that "Satan masquerades as an angel of light."

This is, however, based on conservative thinking and fear because these people refuse to listen to the full depth of the experience, where if we listen with an open mind the full glory of God can be found in these testimonies. In fact, if we also listen with an open heart we may even find that God speaks directly to us through these testimonies.

Together with the power of the experience that we just went through before, the Light in the NDE also holds an experience or sensation of overwhelming love. This is usually the core of the experience and the love that the light, or God, emits is so profound and beyond human comprehension that NDErs cannot find the words to describe it.

It's a kind of love that can't even be explained. It is so hard to explain what being unconditionally loved is...or what it feels like. But it feels like...it feels like the safest, most exalted feeling...ahh...well, you see its ineffable, you run out of words when you try to explain it. But there is no other source that something like that could come from, except some power...and that power is love. Now I call it God.

Here we have the main point: "no other source" than God. Jayne's testimony really goes to the core of the experience and when you add all the things up we have gone through in this chapter then you have a strong case for God. If you take the fact that many of these experiences happen beyond death. And if you take the immense power of the experience and multiply it with the overwhelming sensation of profound love, then you get something truly out of this world: something that could only come from God.

As 80 percent of the people in my study agree with; the profound otherworldly experience of unconditional love in the Light could only have one source, and that source is God.

Based on this, I chose to call this book *The Light Behind God* and this is based on my conviction that the NDE could have been a source of inspiration of religion as we covered in the first chapter. My honest motivation for this is not to destroy any religion or create a new one, but instead to see what religion can learn from the Near Death Experience.

If we are in fact talking about true direct experiences of the source of God, then surely if we are interested in getting closer to God through learning about God, we should listen to these living testimonies. It makes little sense to hold on to outdated words with fear and fight over narrow literal interpretation, if God is alive and well right here, right now.

With this intention, I put my suggestion into my study through the statement: "What I experienced was the core or essence of all religions." Here clearly I was not alone in my conviction as 86 percent said that they either strongly agreed or agreed.

I really feel that the Near Death Experience could have been an early influence on some of the Biblical writers or scholars before Christ, because near death experiences have been with humans as long as there have been humans, and I really think that it's been inspirational. If it's inspirational to us today, it has been inspirational for mankind throughout the ages.

It is clear that if the NDE has happened throughout history as seems very likely from what we went through in the first chapter, then as David just explained it must have been inspirational throughout history as well. And if the NDE was part of religious experience or revelation in the founding days of religion, then the NDE is also a valid source of religion today.

With this in mind, I asked Jayne if she believed that what she experienced is the source of religion, and this was her reply:

I do. I absolutely do, and when I read things about some of the saints or experiences that they have had I think: Aha – very much like an NDE...Absolutely, the story of Paul on the road to Damascus which changed his life and the bright light that he was struck by...After I had my experience and was looking at things in a totally different way; I thought he probably had an NDE.

What Jayne here refers to is Saul's vision that we find in Acts of the Bible. In Acts 22 we have the following testimony from Paul: "I was on my way and approaching Damascus, suddenly about noon there shone round about me a great light from heaven." Paul tells us that this was a dazzling and brilliant light from heaven brighter than the sunshine and clearly something of an otherworldly nature powerful enough to change his life.

Later in Paul's letter to the Galatians, we are told about the nature of Paul's experience and that it is a revelation: "The gospel which was preached to me is not of man. For I did not receive it from man, nor was taught it; but I received it by a revelation."

Clearly with a brilliant light from heaven that revealed the truth directly to Paul and inspired his gospel, we do have many parallels to the NDE, and therefore, it seems reasonable to suggest that the NDE could have been a source of religion. And as mentioned before, this even more so, when we look at the actual universal contents of religion where we find the Golden Rule central to all religions.

David tells us that,

A lot of times when you read some of the older texts; the biblical texts, the Old Testament, there seem to be a lot of parallels in their beliefs; in the Golden Rule and all of that. It just tends to feel very much like the inspiration that you get while you are in the light.

Chapter Three:

The Nature of the Light

In the last chapter we looked at evidence from the Near Death Experience (NDE), which strongly suggests that the Light people experience in their NDE is in fact what religion calls God. And my study found that a majority of 80 percent agreed to call their experience an experience of "God."

However, as we also saw this direct experience of God is to be understood in a very broad sense as a light of God that is spiritually neutral. Based on this it now makes sense to look deeper into the nature of this Light behind God.

The presence; all powerful being, was wonderful, kind and loving. It wasn't like a father or a mother, there was no sense of disappointment or expectation that I had to be someone that I wasn't...I felt it was bigger than anything I had ever known and I mean powerful... Complete love and kindness, totally accepted.

Here Priscilla tells us that God, or what she calls "the presence," is all powerful being and this is a good guide into the nature of the Light behind God. As we also saw earlier, in my study I found that 92 percent agreed that what they experienced was non-physical.

It is very clear from NDE research that God, or the Light, is a non-physical form of energy, which I also confirmed through the finding that 93 percent agreed that "God is a form of energy." Melanie reveals that it is; "a source of energy, like the sun; all knowing, all being, complete," and another testimony tells us that it is: "the source of all; loving, compassion, peace, safety, healing, understanding."

The reason we are talking about something non-physical is that the NDE is an experience of another reality, the realm of God, and this other dimension is very different from our physical world.

Michael explains this as a sphere: "It felt as if I was within a sphere of peace and love. Like the atmosphere of the earth lets me breathe, the sphere lets me feel peace and love. Only the sphere had no limit of scope."

Also Jim's testimony points us in this direction as he reveals that,

> I just experienced this incredible loving light and I was just in awe of it because there wasn't anything outside of it. That light contained the universe. It contained all the phenomena and all the non-phenomena. There wasn't anything that wasn't that light.

As NDE research generally finds this is beyond human comprehension because the amount of information that each person receives outside the body cannot be contained in the body or mind here on earth. But still in my study I wanted to get closer to what this nature is through multiple-choice.

Like Michael described his experience as the experience of a sphere of peace I found that 66 percent would use the words "absolute peace" to describe their experience. Chris S. tells us that, "It was a welcoming, loving place in which you could sense God light."

Moving further with the word "compassion," I found a higher score of 87 percent who agreed to call the light compassionate. Connie reveals the experience as: "It was absolute compassion and understanding and respect for who we are. We are absolutely respected and loved beyond human understanding. We are cherished to the core."

When using the word "absolute love" I found that 80 percent agreed to use this description, and by using absolute it is very clear that we are talking about a different kind of love than the love we usually mean here on earth. The kind of love that NDErs experience is difficult to explain as Jacqui tells us it's an "amazing love and beauty that is hard to explain...light, love, beauty, clarity, warmth, a higher meaning."

The higher meaning of this love makes it of another world as an unearthly love that is much more strong or powerful than the love many of us feel here on earth. Mary reveals that it is the "love of God" and that this is an "unearthly unconditional Love," which is "a million times stronger than any earthly experience and was different in that it was total and unconditional."

Being unearthly and unconditional also makes people describe this as a love that is pure in its form, and in my study I found that 87 percent agreed to call the Light "pure love." Here Paul tells us that "All was light; All was Love," and he gives us this explanation about the nature of the light, where he describes his experience of pure love and what he calls "True Love":

I saw the beautiful and strong light. It was more beautiful than our words; it was brighter than anything I had ever seen but did not 'blind' me; the Love was greater than anything I had ever experienced...It was pure light and pure LOVE...True Love; True Reality.

Along with this strong sense of pure or true love people who have NDEs also generally note upon a strong sensation of oneness. I found that 93 percent said that they had the "experience of oneness," and 80 percent said that they agreed with the statement: "All is one."

This oneness is usually described as the interconnectedness of all things. Dave explains that, "I felt a connection to everything. That would include anything that has ever been, is, or ever will be...everything."

To confirm Dave's testimony, in my study I found total consensus with 100 percent agreeing to the statement: "We are all interconnected; all life shares the same essence."

Also, another NDEr, David remarks upon this sense of interconnectedness as he tells us that the core of his experience was; "LOVE and interconnectedness" and that this love was: "Acceptance, Tolerance, Truth, Infinite Knowing, Home and Welcoming."

And David gives this longer explanation of just how powerful the sense of love is in the NDE:

I experienced incredible Love and knowledge beyond my true being while in the light. The Love was so powerful that you cannot compare it to this physical world. If we were to experience it while in this body it would overwhelm our senses to a point of incapacitation.

As religion tells us that God is love the NDE agrees very much with this point as being the essence of the Light or God. Paul tells us that, "God is Real. God is Love," and from Jacqui we can learn that: "Love is the most important thing in life and without love you have nothing."

Based on this, and on NDE research in general, if we try to explain the nature of the Light or God in one word; this word would be: Love. That is what people experience as the core and true nature of the Light and this is the most important message from the NDE.

P. M. H. Atwater explains that,

There is a message for everyone. If you are going to say that there is one message then you would have to say that that message is love. If you are going to concentrate everything down into one feeling, one power, one sense of what it's all about and who we are, it would be the word "love."

However, the message does not stop there since it goes further as Atwater tells us that, "We are divine beings having a human experience...we are co-creators with the creator." The implication of this is that we are here to create love: If God is love and we are co-creators with the creator, then we are here to create love with the creator.

This is why NDErs conclude that the Golden Rule is an indisputable law of the universe in their NDEs, and why most people report significant positive life-changes after their experience. As explained people become more loving, compassionate, tolerant, forgiving and kind to others, and these positive changes in attitude towards others are seen as an authentic response to the nature of the Light – to the nature of God.

These fruits of the NDE come from the extreme power of the unconditional love felt while in the Light, and the fact that many people make significant changes to their lives is a testimony to how strong the reality of this love is felt.

In my study I found that 92 percent said that they agreed with the statement: "We need to learn to love each other." I also asked about the statement: "The world needs to learn the Golden Rule and respect all life," and here I found that 77 percent agreed.

Chris confirms this need based on his conclusion from his experience where he explains that, "What I got from this is that we are for sure, without a doubt, our brother's and sister's keeper. Absolutely. That's the whole reason we are here. That's the truth."

Chris bases this conclusion on the message he received in his NDE:

The message from the voice during my flashback was about our interconnection with others; what we meant to them. In that sense we feel the value of ourselves for being part of the web of life, and the continued efforts to teach love. As we learn to love others at a deeper level, and have respect and love for all life, we ascend to higher thought levels.

As here explained, it is the lesson learned from the flashback in the life-review that we find in the NDE. And as we saw this ultimate teaching tool leads NDErs to conclude that the Golden Rule is an indisputable law of the universe.

Being love and creating love through the Golden Rule is the whole reason that we are here.

However, this doesn't necessarily mean that we have to do big things as one NDEr tells us that, "It's the little things in life which count. The simple acts of kindness towards others. Kindness and forgiveness of our-selves is important."

Also Priscilla explains that: "Just be kind to all," and from Jim we learn that this can be as simple as just "being totally present" in the moment. This can be with family members or strangers we meet on the street and we can understand this being present in the moment as loving our neighbor.

In fact, due to the experience of oneness and interconnectedness in the NDE we could conclude that our sense of separateness is an illusion. This I had confirmed in my study where 83 percent said that they agreed to the statement: "There is no other; we are the other."

This is where religious saints come in as sources of inspiration. We may not all have the same spiritual power as e.g. Mother Theresa, but saints like her remind us of how deep and profound the love of God really is.

Also in the Christian religion we find that in the Bible the loving and compassionate actions of Jesus inspire us towards a deeper love than what is usually expressed in our world. It is these kinds of compassionate actions and the burning heart of Jesus as the Prince of Peace, that really resonate with the true nature of the Light and the deep love of God.

In *Lessons from the Light*, researcher Kenneth Ring explains that there is a clear link between religious teachings and what people experience in the Light of the NDE:

Those who are blessed enough to travel there [into the Light] are the persons who are perhaps best equipped to express for us what might fairly be called the "ultimate lessons of the Light," form which, using a phrase associated with the world's great spiritual traditions, the essential "wisdom teachings" of the NDE can be extracted.

A personal favorite quote of mine expressing the ultimate lessons of the Light is: "All we have is what we give" – meaning that all we have in truth is the love that we give to others. As a researcher, I believe this one line is the closest we can get to express the profound love of the Light in human language. It is at the same time also a powerful testimony to how saints and religious figures like Jesus lived their lives, and I firmly believe this shows us that we are indeed talking about the same source.

The reason we love and remember these people is based on their powerful ability to love and give, and us knowing that they did not waste a moment to do so. The Bible also states this in 1 John 3:18-20: "Let us love, not in words or speech, but in truth and action...for God is greater than our hearts."

It is especially the last part that "God is greater than our hearts," which the NDE gives testimony to as the profound infinite love of the Light is beyond human comprehension. As NDErs will say; beyond their ability to describe their experience, they will also say that this profound love of the Light, God, is beyond human comprehension and greater than our human hearts.

In my study, I had this notion confirmed through the statement: "Human understanding of God is far from the true nature of love," where 71 percent said that they agreed. This is not meant to talk down to religious people, as I also found that the rest, 29 percent, said that they were "not sure," but the aim here was to show that the true nature of God's love is beyond our human comprehension.

Besides a powerful message that calls on us to love, we also find a strong sense of purpose in the NDE – a reason why we are here on earth. Jacqui tells us that there is a "higher meaning; we are on earth as humans to learn lessons."

This was also something that Raymond Moody concluded from his research. The life-review stresses the importance of "learning to love," and from the late long time hospice worker, Elisabeth Kubler-Ross we get the same conclusion: "The sole purpose of life is to grow. The ultimate lesson is learning to love and be loved *unconditionally*."

While love here on earth many times is conditional, the kind of love experienced in the Light and as the true nature of God, is unconditional beyond comprehension. In the light there is an experience of total freedom and this freedom comes from the unconditional love of the Light.

My wife, Valerie, was actually the person who made me aware of this link when she told me: "Unconditional love sets you free because you are totally accepted." This means that there is no fear what so ever in unconditional love, which is also something we can learn in the Bible 1 John 4:18:

There is no fear in love. But perfect love drives out fear, because fear has to do with punishment. The one who fears is not made perfect in love.

Both fear and punishment has here nothing to do with love, as the Bible tells us God's love is perfect and the NDE reveals this love is unconditional. This is an important insight from the NDE that will become clearer throughout the book.

In relation to learning to love and be loved, I also found something important in my study. To the statement, "The true nature of reality is love; we are here to learn who we are," I found that 69 percent said that they agreed.

This brings us to an important point that Kenneth Ring also arrived at in *Lessons from the Light*. He explains that, "The absolute and unconditional love of the Light reveals the essence of the individual's true self."

This is an important insight from the Light that we will look at throughout the book, but for now I wish to conclude that because; "Love is everything and everything is love," as David testifies, this also means that we are love. Everything has an essence of love, and as such our essence and true nature is also love.

Chapter Four:

Death and Resurrection

As we looked at in chapter two, near death experiences (NDEs) that happen when people are clinically dead go beyond death, and therefore, it is no wonder that people who have NDEs are convinced that life continues after death.

Michael tells us that, "One thing that resounds unendingly through every vibration of my experience is that we never really die...that we will live on after this life."

Also Connie explains the message from her NDE was that life is eternal and that we have a true home somewhere else:

> *To me, the message was that we are much more than our bodies, that life is eternal, that we are held in Divine loving arms at all times, that we are respected and cherished, that we are powerful beings, that life on earth is only temporary and that only a small part of our consciousness resides in these bodies. That we are One with each other and with God, that all understanding is available to us, that we are operating at a dense, lower, slower vibration right now but that there is a much higher vibration which is our true Home.*

In my study I asked the NDErs about the statement, "Life is eternal; I have absolutely no doubt about that," to which 93 percent said that they agreed. This consensus reflects one of the most convincing conclusions from the NDE; that life continues.

However, the full implication of what NDErs are saying about death is even bigger than that. I found that eight out of ten would agree to the statement; "We don't have a life; we are eternal life," and this tells us that the idea of death as the end of life in the form of nothingness is not real.

Based on her extensive research, P. H. M. Atwater gave this explanation:

The number one phrase that near death experiencers say when they come back is four words. It doesn't matter the country they are saying the same four words and those four words are: "always there is life. Always there is life." If you really hang with that, think about that, let it shift in and through your body; then that is saying that there is no such thing as an afterlife. There is no such thing as a before life. The only reality is that always there is life. In some form, in some dimension, in some realm, in some place; always you are alive.

Together with this overwhelming conviction that life is eternal we naturally find a complete loss of the fear of dying. After having an NDE people are no longer afraid of dying, and in fact, most people even look forward to death as a joyous experience as Dave here reveals: "I have no fear of what is to come. Personally, I can't wait, like being a kid; it's Wednesday and on Friday we get to go to Disneyland."

The Disneyland that Dave talks about is the joy and peace coming from the Light that many people find so pleasant that they do not want to come back to this world again. The love coming from the Light is so profound and deep that many people do not want to return to this life again.

There was only peace. No pain, strife, anger, or anything negative...Death is not something to be afraid of, not because it's an illusion, but because it's a transition from one state to another.

What Michael here testifies is that in the transition from this world to the other side, our state of being is also transformed into another state of being. This means that on the other side there is no pain, even if people are in pain due to the dying process or an accident, in the transition they will be liberated from this pain.

People who are suffering before they have their NDE testify that their pain is replaced by a wonderful feeling of peace and joy, and that there is no reason to fear the moment of crossing over even if the process of dying is painful. The journey to the other side through the transition into another state is so overwhelmingly blissful that all pain and sorrow disappears completely.

Another fear people have about dying is the pain of leaving loved ones behind. Here we can also learn a great insight from the NDE:

It was the most natural thing in the world...I was ready to go toward the light and I went toward the light. I kind of beat myself up over that for a while when I came back. Because while I was in the Light I didn't want to come back and when I came back I was like: I had a family here. I had a wife I left behind. Why wasn't I worried about that? I felt like I should have wanted to return for them. Instead I wanted to stay in the Light because it seemed like the most loving, the most welcoming, most compassionate thing that I had ever experienced. And I had no thought of them.

Here David tells us about his own guilt of not thinking of his family while in the Light, but he also reveals an important insight from the NDE. While of course the people we leave behind in death will feel pain and sorrow about their loss, people who have NDEs mostly let go of any attachment to this world including the attachment to loved ones.

The reason for this is as David explains; the love and warmth coming from the Light, but it is also because the journey to the other side is a profound transition into another, much larger, sense of reality. As we saw, the other dimension is far more real than this world, and as such, it has a much bigger sense of meaning.

This sense of higher meaning together with the feeling of profound love and peace results in a shift in focus away from this world and towards the Light – our new world – and through these positive sensations in the transition we can find great support and help in letting go.

While loved ones left behind still feel the loss, the transition for the dying person is in the end a very personal experience and through this understanding, it can also be easier for those of us left behind to let go.

"I believe my experience was meant to teach me that we are much more than our bodies." Here Connie explains that we are much more than our bodies, as souls or spiritual beings, which is often the conclusion that we find in the NDE. Russ tells us the same about his experience that, "This causes me to believe that rather than my body having a soul, I am my soul and I have a body as my earthly vehicle."

Also we find in the NDE there is a clear sense that life continues without our physical bodies as Michael here explains:

>The Truth of the experience was self-evident to me. The Truth that God Is, that death is not the end, that we are eternal and that when our physical bodies no longer function, we continue to exist without them. This Truth was self-evident.

That we are souls, or spiritual beings, is an insight from the NDE that speaks to the Christian idea of the Resurrection as the resurrection of the physical body. Most people knowing the laws of nature would agree that the physical body decays, however, this does not mean that we cannot be resurrected as a spiritual body.

As an "earthly vehicle" we can conclude that the body will decay according to the laws of nature, but also through NDE research we can learn that we continue to live on as "spiritual bodies." However, we can also learn something rather interesting and very important about this spiritual existence from people who have been there.

In my study I found that 92 percent agreed to the statement: "What I experienced was non-physical" and thereby most NDErs in my study clearly disagree that their experience is physical. Also the fact that most people in their NDE actually leave their body tells us something. The

Out-of-Body experience is very common to the NDE and in this experience people are able to look down, often from the corner of the hospital room, and then see their own body from the outside.

After leaving the body and going through the transition to the other side, NDErs will often say that they felt like "a spectator," or even "a third person," because they are able to observe their body and activities around them from a distance.

Raymond Moody calls this having a "spiritual body" because the NDEr has clearly left the physical body. Having left the body and knowing that NDErs have the experience that we are able to exist without the body, the question then becomes what we continue to exist as?

One answer I got from my study was consciousness. I asked whether "consciousness was at the center" of the experience, and here I found that 86 percent said that they agreed. What this means is that as we have clinically dead people with clear consciousness, and people who leave their body with the experience of consciousness as their center without their physical body.

About the soul as this center of consciousness one NDEr explains that,

Us Catholics we knew about the soul being different from the body, but the soul was this little thing inside of you and when you died this little thing came out. No, it's

exactly the opposite. The soul is much bigger. All of this is just a wrapper for the soul and the soul is us, the "I-ness." I was still Chris when I was there and reviewing the movie. I was still Chris. So the soul is this big huge thing.

Here Chris clearly defines the center of his experience, his soul, as the "I-ness" and this supports the conclusion of consciousness as the center of the experience. Also Moody found that some people did not feel like they were in any kind of body at all, since they felt more like they were "pure consciousness" as a point of awareness.

These experiences of the afterlife outside the body and as a spiritual body, also tell us something important about the dogmatic view of the Resurrection as the resurrection of the physical body. If we really want to know about what happens when we die, then this insight that we are resurrected as a spiritual body and that consciousness is at the center of this experience, is very important.

On the Resurrection and the understanding of this as the resurrection of the physical body, Carl Jung once had this to say:

To the primitive Christians as to all primitives, the Resurrection had to be a concrete, materialistic event to be seen by the eyes and touched by the hands, as if the spirit had no existence of its own.

In "earth to earth and dust to dust" it is of course clear that we cannot take the body with us as it rots and turns back into earth. This materialistic understanding of the Resurrection can also be found with the ancient Egyptians. In the *Egyptian Book of the Dead* we find that the soul – "ba" – also has a physical aspect because it lives in the heart – "ka" – and the *ba* cannot live without this physical home, the *ka*.

This is partly clear through the preservation of the body through embalmment. However, the climate in Egypt also had an impact on this tradition as the intense heart would make the body decay much faster without the mummification. Whatever the reason, it seems pretty clear that the Egyptians where confusing the material things of the body with the immaterial of the soul.

Whether Christianity inherited this confusion about the Resurrection from the Egyptians or some other source is difficult to say for sure, but certain is it that the Bible does not only talk about the Resurrection as a physical event. In fact, there are plenty of biblical references to the Resurrection as a spiritual body like people experience in the NDE.

In Galatians 6:8 we are told that, "he who sows in the flesh, from the flesh also will reap corruption. But, he who sows in the spirit, form the spirit will reap life everlasting." And in 1 Corinthians 15:50 we find that: "I declare to you, brothers, that flesh and blood cannot inherit the Kingdom of God, nor does the perishable inherit the imperishable."

Also John tells us the same in verse 3:5 that, "No one can enter the Kingdom of God unless he is born of water and spirit. Flesh gives birth to flesh, but the Spirit gives birth to spirit."

To further explain this, in John 3:8 we are even given a metaphor and a parable of Jesus about the spirit: "The wind blows wherever it pleases. You hear its sound, but you cannot tell where it comes from or where it is going. So it is with everyone born of the Spirit."

With the wind as a metaphor for the spirit it is clear that we are not talking about a physical thing, and in 1 Corinthians 15:40 we also find the distinction between the physical body and spiritual body is made clear:

> There are also heavenly bodies and there are earthly bodies; but the splendor of the heavenly bodies is one kind, and the splendor of the earthly bodies is another...So will it be with the resurrection of the dead. The body that is sown is perishable, it is raised imperishable; it is sown a natural body, it is raised a spiritual body.

While some Christians get stuck with the literal interpretation of the Resurrection, by looking a little deeper we do find in the Bible that we are "raised a spiritual body," which fits perfectly with what people experience in the NDE.

Jayne reveals that:

There is absolutely no reason to fear death. Death is simply the closing of one door and the opening of another. You simply leave your physical, worn out or disease ridden body, and go into a different dimension of consciousness where you don't need a body because you are in a spiritual realm at that point. It's actually...if someone is really ill and tired and worn out it must be wonderful to leave that body behind and go into this other realm.

To understand why most NDErs have absolutely no fear of death, we should remember the sheer power and intensity of the experience that we looked at in the last chapter. Here 78 percent said that the sensation was stronger than here on earth and two thirds said that the experience was more than 100 percent real.

When you add this strong sense of a higher reality to the power of conviction, it is no wonder that NDErs are able to say like Jayne: "*Knowing* that there is no death, not hoping, not praying for it, but not being afraid of anything anymore because there is no death."

However, while knowing that there is no death and not being afraid of death itself Jayne also reveals something critical about death:

I did think at that time that the most important part of the experience was learning that there is no death...It took a few decades before I realized that looking into my soul and seeing that I was love was equally as important...possibly even more so, I don't know...but equally as important as knowing that there was no death; was knowing what I was, who I was; who we all are.

Knowing that life continues and that there is no reason to fear death on this side is one thing, but being able to meet the sheer power of the Light and embrace the full glory of God in the other dimension is another thing.

This is an important insight about the afterlife that NDE research reveals and something that we will look into throughout the book, especially in chapter nine.

Chapter Five:

The Light is Not Angry

As we just went through in the last chapter, the nature of the Light is love beyond human comprehension and as we find in religion, people who have Near Death Experiences (NDEs) also say that God is love. In my study I found that 93 percent said that they agreed with the statement "God is love."

But how are we to understand this love? Are we talking about conditional love, unconditional love or something in between? This is a very divisive question in religion and a source of conflict, but it is an area where the Near Death Experience (NDE) has a very important message for religion and the world:

There is no such thing as an angry God. The God force or power that I felt was totally forgiving of any so-called error. In my wildest dreams I cannot conceive of God being interested in punishing. God is interested in bringing us to 'him' – to love. Punishment just isn't God's game...It's not who God is, it's not what God is. God is all loving, all forgiving, all accepting.

Jayne's testimony is standard to NDE research and to the statement "God is angry" I found one of the highest levels of consensus in my study with 100 percent saying they disagreed with the statement. Almost eight out of ten, 78 percent, said that they strongly disagreed with the statement based on the experience that God is not angry and this is a key message that people bring back from the Light.

I put the question whether there is any evidence of an angry God in NDE research to P.M.H. Atwater:

I have yet to hear of any experiencer, adult or child, that spoke of an angry God or a God that was upset, or in any way anything but loving and accepting and forgiving. However, I have heard many times of the various greeters that come to greet people once they have crossed over to the other side. Some of those can be quite critical. Some of those can be quite strict. Some of those can be rather frightening. Some of those can be like demonic...But as far as the one great light, what you and I would call God; no. Nothing negative, nothing horrific, no anger, no judgment.

I included the long answer in the beginning of this chapter not to confuse some readers. It is true that in NDE research we do find negative experiences, or so-called distressing experiences, which happen to about 15 percent of people who have NDEs.

We also find that hellish experiences, which are described as "truly hellish" happen to about one third of this group and to approximately 5 percent of people who have an NDE. These hell-like experiences can be frightening or even demonic in nature as Atwater explains, and based on this one could jump to the conclusion that this is evidence that God is angry.

But things are not that simple as the full understanding of the NDE takes a deeper investigation. Just because people have negative or hellish experiences it does not automatic follow that God is angry. The important distinction here is the separation between the Light or God and what Atwater calls the "greeters" in the negative experiences. In NDE research we find a clear separation between the Light and the negative experiences.

This is of course supported by the fact that NDErs tell us that God is love and not angry, but also through the fact that even the people who have negative or distressing experiences, will say that on a whole their experience was positive.

In my study I found that all the people, 100 percent, who had distressing elements in their experience, said that the experience on a whole was positive. I also found the same high level of consensus among the NDErs against the statement: "God wants to punish us in hell." Here 100 percent said that they disagreed, with 85 percent saying that they strongly disagreed with the statement.

What this points to is the conclusion that the greeter or the negative experience is not the true nature of the Light. For NDErs there is a clear sense that the negative experience and the judgment does not come from the Light or from God.

My experience was of all embracing love, light, acceptance, and I guarantee you on this earth I have not lived the perfect life. But in that space, place, beingness, I was totally accepted and part of it and at one with it. So there was no judgment.

As Cheryl here explains the Light is all embracing love and acceptance with no judgment. This is the nature of the Light and when we do find judgment in the NDE it seems to come not from the Light but from the person themself:

I did not experience any anger. In my life-review, I experienced a lot of things that I was judging – me – the humanness that came along with me that I hadn't quite shed yet. Because I think dying is a process and I think that when we re-integrate into that light, it takes a while to distill some of our attitudes and leave it behind. I think we bring some of it with us for a while and I was judging my life's experiences but my soul family wasn't. There was no judgment in this light. I was ashamed that they had to experience some of the unsavory things that I had done. But they weren't, they weren't judging it. They were experiencing it.

Here David clearly has a sense that the judgment was coming from him-self, or as he explains; the humanness he brought along with him into the Light caused him to feel ashamed about his actions that he reviewed in his life-review.

This experience is general to NDE research and Dr. Bruce Greyson, who has been a researcher for over 30 years, explains that:

Most people don't have a sense of judgment but those that do usually say that they were judging themselves; that they were guided through a life-review by some type of an unconditional loving being and they themselves felt guilty about disappointing this being or just disappointing themselves.

The distinction between the Light as unconditional non-judgmental love and then our own judgment can be very hard for some people to understand.

In sharing my research, I often receive emails from people that strongly object to the finding that God is not angry. It is easy to label these people fundamentalists and reject them, but as a researcher I try to understand their concerns by listening to their arguments.

Here is one message that I received from a person that I will keep anonymous:

I think the Light of God is conscious, not just a blob of unconditional love, it is consciousness and aware and being love and wisdom, and would not want anyone to suffer. Most don't penetrate the light but I am sure it is more aware than any human awareness and represents holiness and goodness, which means it is automatically opposed to evil, cruelty, sin, and abuse.

I included this e-mail because I think it contains a valid question: how can God seemly be unconscious in the face of cruelty and abuse? I do not think that NDE research agrees with the logical conclusion that because the Light of God is conscious, therefore it is also automatically opposed to evil. Automatically clearly suggest being actively opposed, or as the person explains further: "Part of love is holiness and justice, and I don't think God is sitting back indifferent to evil."

The first assumption here is that because NDErs testify that God is unconditional love, therefore God is unconscious and indifferent to cruelty and abuse. This assumption is based on the lack of distinction between God and the negative experiences – the crucial separation – that we looked at in the beginning of the chapter. Just because God is unconditional non-judgmental love, it does not follow that there are no consequences towards cruelty and abuse.

Clearly since people do have negative and distressing experiences that can be very powerful in their frightening or painful nature, it is not a free ride to God. The important distinction here is that while NDErs do have negative experiences these do not seem to originate from the Light or God.

If we interpret the negative experiences as a consequence, it is fair to conclude that there are consequences in our journey to God. But again, the crucial distinction is that there can be consequences without these consequences being a punishment.

Also it could even be possible that these consequences are not God's intention or doing. We have to remember that we all have free will, and as such, it seems unreasonable to pin everything that happens on God.

Edward who grew up with an image of a judgmental God testifies that,

In my experience, sitting literally in the lap of God, I was directed to look at my life like so many pictures on the floor from a photo album that had been dropped. I would look at my life and remember experiences and I would relive these experiences, some of which I was very

ashamed of...But I didn't have a sense of judgment other than allowing me to know that there are consequences to my behavior. But there are no emotional attachments from my creator as to how I respond.

Here Edward clearly tells us that there can be consequences to our behavior without a sense of judgment and this is the general crucial distinction that we find in NDE research. However, this testimony goes further than that and explains that there are no emotional attachments from the creator – there is no anger coming from God – as to how we respond.

Now, if we go back to the person that was convinced that God is actively opposed to cruelty and abuse, there is no other area as controversial as war. In our history we see clear evidence of the danger to religion when God is mixed with militarism and even in our supposedly enlightened times this militant aspect of religion, or specifically some followers of religion, is still alive and well.

Today, we have suicide bombers on one side believing that killing innocent people gives them instant access to heaven, while on the other side we believe that God is so angry at one particular dictator that God chooses to look the other way when innocent civilians are killed in 'his' name.

I believe it is wise to clean your own house first, and since the start of the war in Iraq I have been both shocked and puzzled how polls could show that nearly 90 percent of white so-called born again Christians in the US could support the war. And if you looked at the 31 percent of Americans that believe in an angry God, you could also find overwhelming support for the war with two out of three Americans.

Knowing about this strong support for war among certain Christians and wanting to know more, I put this to the person with whom I had an e-mail exchange on this topic:

I supported the war to remove Saddam and I still do. He was a brutal dictator who ruled his people with fear and bloodshed, and his sons were even more psychopathic. If anyone studies just how evil Saddam was their opposition to his removal would end. God is merciful and patient, but when the abuse and sin becomes intentional and without repentance or conscience then God does step in and remove it and does not allow evil to enter heaven.

We have here the strong sense of God actively taking action and even stepping in to "remove" the "evil." This is what the person meant about God being conscious and thus acting through us. If God is in everything, then it does make sense to say that God acts through us. And as Jesus did in his life, it is natural to conclude that God would protect the weak and defenseless, but we have to remember that innocent people were killed in the process.

There are no precise figures of how many civilians have been killed in Iraq, since the US army has learned not to count "collateral damage" after the Vietnam War because it is bad press when people see the consequences of war. But the death toll is estimated somewhere between one hundred thousand and one million people, with one hundred thousand civilians being the most conservative.

I will just point out some facts from the most recent war in order to show just how far some believers are able to take their faith in God.

On October 2, 2002, Richard D. Land, President of the Ethics and Religious Liberty Commission at the Southern Baptist Convention along with three other ministers, send the so-called "Land Letter" to George W. Bush. The letter argued for a just war against Iraq based on the fear of Hitler argument, and on the question of proportionality; if the good gained by resorting to armed conflict would "justify the cost of lives" the letter said:

> We believe that the cost of not dealing with this threat now will only succeed in greatly increasing the cost in human lives and suffering when an even more heavily armed and dangerous Saddam Hussein most be confronted at some date in the not too distant future.

Two months later *Christianity Today* published an article titled *Just War in Iraq* by one of the co-signing ministers, Charles Colson, which concluded that, "Out of love of neighbor, then, Christians can and should support a preemptive strike, if ordered by the appropriate magistrate to prevent an imminent attack."

Whether it was the call to action by these evangelical leaders or they were just following the mood of the country I am not sure. But in April 2003 after the invasion the New York Times reported that 87 percent of white evangelical Christians said they supported the decision to go to war. Almost three years later in 2006 after no weapons of mass destruction, no links to Al-Qaida, and horrible losses in human lives, polls still showed that 68 percent continued their support.

Can we really kill in the name of God and still be at one with God? And this when our arguments are based on fear and ignorance?

I asked the NDErs in my study about the following statement: "To kill in the name of God is far from the true nature of God." Here an overwhelming majority of 92 percent said that they agreed, with three out of four saying that they strongly agreed.

When we say "God" and the Muslims say "Allah" we are all talking about that same source. But we don't interpret it all the same because the kind of love that I felt would never ever permit killing for the sake of this love. Anytime I hear of anything about the war it breaks my heart and I am thinking to myself: guys it's not the way.

Here Jayne tells us that God would never want us to kill for the sake of love or in the name of God, which is the overwhelming conclusion from near death experiences. The love of God experienced in the NDE is so profound and its respect for life is so deep that it very clearly seems not to be able to kill and also would not endorse killing.

However, as we saw earlier, alongside these testimonies of profound love we still do have painful consequences through the negative experiences, so when God is love; then how are we to understand these consequences?

Mary explains that, "Love and truth are undivided; they are equal aspects of The Light, or God." With this statement in mind, I wanted to go deeper into this apparent paradox by asking each NDEr to describe what the truth in their experience was based on the question: "How would you describe the element of truth at the core of your experience?"

Here 80 percent marked the words "truth" and "enlightenment," while only 13 percent said "judgment" and 20 percent said "justice." And moving deeper into judgment as, "blame" or "guilt" I found that only 6 percent used this definition.

Getting away from the idea of truth as judgment or punishment, I found that 60 percent said that the element of truth in their experience wanted to "teach" or "show me the way," and 73 percent said that the Light was "teaching me with love and compassion."

Clearly the non-judgmental unconditional love of the Light is not experienced as a punishment, but as what is most commonly found in NDE research; the Light wants us to learn as we grow our soul.

To back this up 69 percent said that they agreed with "God does not punish" and the same amount, nearly seven out of ten, said that they disagreed with "God uses stick and carrot." By 'stick and carrot' is meant the usual method of motivation through punishment and reward that we find in society, but as found in my study and general to NDE research; NDErs do not experience a reward-punishment crisis in the Light.

Jayne explains here how she as an NDEr looks upon punishment in religion:

The punishing God seems to be that of the Old Testament and I think that was Jesus' mission to come and raise our consciousness into this other way of knowing God – the real God. Prior to that man made God is his image but we just can't do that to God because that is not who God is.

If God is love and does not punish then we will have to look for a different source of this urge to punish. Again I will let our anonymous person speak for the side of punishment: "If you knew anything about how cruel Saddam was you would realize the loving thing it was to take action through self sacrifice to free the people from his brutalization."

There are two major points here. First we have that the belief in a loving God does not see or "realize" the full extent of the cruelty. From this point of view, taking action to free the people is done out of love as "self sacrifice" even though a shocking amount of eggs were broken in the process.

Secondly, overlooking the killing of a horrific number of innocent people means that the end justifies the means and this process is called "creative destruction." Creative destruction is not very compassionate because it destroys in its effort to create, and when militarism is looking towards God for an alibi, religion can end up in bad company.

The question is whether a God that is love really seeks order through active destruction? Or maybe a more balanced and harmonious form of creation that includes a love for our neighbor, which also respects his or her right to live as an end in it-self? Obviously, nature and the universe is a violent place but is this also the true nature of God?

With this question in mind, I wanted to see how a just God rated against a loving God: "Justice is more important to God than love or compassion." Firmly based on the experience that God is love 93% said that they disagreed. And to the statement: "Forgiveness is more important than justice," I found that 71 percent said that they agreed.

What we are getting at here is the common distinction between the Old Testament and the New Testament of the Bible that Jayne just pointed out. While an angry God is often found in the Old Testament, if one takes the words of Jesus to heart and interpret them according to how he lived his life – walked his talk – then we are getting closer to what the Light in the NDE is trying to tell us.

Most of us will admit that human emotions such as fear and anger, do not always lead to enlightened or compassionate actions. Also there is a clear paradox between a relentless fight against "evil" and the teachings of religion that God is love, because if we are always fighting there is no time to love and there can be no peace.

In the late 19th century Biblical scholar of Hebrew, Robertson Smith, gave a series of lectures that were published as *The Religion of the Semites* and he explained that,

However true it is that savage man feels himself to be environed by innumerable dangers which he does not understand and so personifies as invisible or mysterious enemies of more than human power, it is not true that the

attempt to appease these powers is the foundation of religion.

Robertson makes the argument based on his field studies in the holy land, which found that it is only in times of social dissolution that we find that God is angry. Therefore, as he explains above; the constant active attempt to fight against "evil" is not the foundation of religion. This was an important statement, something that the living testimonies of God in the NDE supports and something that the world still needs to learn.

Logically there is a clear parallel between a so-called "war against terror" and a fight against "evil," and one could ask whether this black and white, either/or, logic comes from God or from man?

In the history of philosophy we find that the concept of true and false originate from late Greek and Roman thinking, something that some philosophers believe served the Roman Empire well as it took over most of the known world. It is obvious if you seek to impose your will on others that claiming to hold the only truth and aggressively rejecting the opposite is a good tool for control.

However, if we go back to the ancient Greeks we do not find false as opposed to true. Here false means to "bring to ruin" or to "make unsteady," and truth here is not aligned opposite to false in a way that would inspire opposition as what we find in Latin *falsum*.

In her book *Purity and Danger* Mary Douglas tells us that,

> *The final paradox of the search for purity is that it is an attempt to force experience into logical categories of non-contradiction. But experience is not amenable and those who make the attempt find themselves led into contradiction...Whenever a strict pattern of purity is imposed on our lives it is either highly uncomfortable or it leads into contradiction if closely followed leads to hypocrisy.*

Here Douglas explains that our extreme search for purity in which we force the rejection of the unclean, or "evil," will not only lead us into contradiction but also hypocrisy. An area where this hypocrisy clearly comes out is the abortion debate in the US. While people against abortion call themselves "pro-life" their hypocrisy comes to light through their alliance with the Republican Party and support for war. The standard argument is that while war is sometimes justified, abortion is always morally wrong.

Pro-life and pro-war is a contradiction that is often found among right wing Christians in the US, and when these same people try to interpret the words of Jesus to support war, the contradiction becomes even more apparent.

Taken out of context it is possible to find evidence for most things in the Bible, and some people will see the turning over of the tables of the money changes in front of the temple as Jesus' endorsement of conflict. Or when Jesus talks about bringing a truth that will divide families, the word "sword" and "not to bring peace" are taken literally to mean war.

However, this interpretation taken out of context is much too simple for a great person like Jesus, and we should give his teachings more credit than that. Instead of jumping to conclusion and if we look at the facts about Jesus through the life of Jesus; from his actions and how he walked his talk we can see a different interpretation emerge.

Jesus was living in a time of Roman occupation, and yet he said that those who live by the sword will die by the sword. Rather than a violent uprising against Rome he called for a spiritual revolution from within as he came to bring peace.

Many Christians today know that the Jews did not accept or recognize Jesus as their Messiah, but only few know that about a hundred years after Jesus the Jews did actually believe that they had found their Messiah. During the second Jewish Revolt in 132 – 135 AD, the Jewish rebel leader Bar Kokhba was proclaimed to be the Messiah of the Jewish people.

The reason not many know about this is that Bar Kokhba's messianic status was recanted after the Romans violently crushed the rebellion causing devastating losses on both sides, and the belief in militarism brought immense bloodshed to the Jewish people.

This was not the only revolt and not the only time a Messiah was proclaimed, and Jesus was very aware of the politics of the time that he was living in. Therefore, to realize his message it is helpful to understand this underlying struggle against Rome as the backdrop of his ministry.

Upon Jesus' triumphal entry to Jerusalem we are told that he weeps over the state of the city as he clearly sees things to come.

Luke testifies in Chapter 19:42-44 that:

If you had only known today what could have brought you peace! But now it is hidden from your sight, because the days will come when your enemies will build walls around you, surround you, and close in on every side. They will level you to the ground and kill your people. One stone will not be left on top of another, because you didn't recognize the time when God came to help you.

It is very easy to take one line out of context, but if we look at the history and politics of the time of Jesus, it is hard to make the case for war in the name of Christ. As the Jewish people, Jesus would have had plenty of reason and occasion to fight violently against Rome, if he was politically motivated and it was this kind of revolution that he was talking about.

But the indisputable fact of how he lived his life shows us how to understand his teaching. In Matthew chapter 24

Jesus even warns us that many will come in his name saying; "I am the Christ" and that many will be led astray: "For you shall hear of wars and rumors of wars. Take care that you do not be alarmed, for these things must come to pass."

I believe that the living testimonies that we have today from the Light behind God through research of NDEs, weighs heavy in support of the interpretation of Jesus as the Prince of Peace and a Lamb of God.

I think religious people who support war or resistance in the name of God should at least try to listen to these testimonies from a living God, before they jump to the conclusion that God is angry. Just because we humans get angry it does not follow that God therefore also must be angry.

If it were so, then there would be nothing to look up to, nothing to hold sacred, and nothing to be inspired by. As people experience in the NDE, the Light is greater than what we can perceive and comprehend, so God must ultimately be something to look up to – something greater than our human hearts and minds.

Chapter Six:

Adam's Alibi

In the last chapter, we arrived at the conclusion that God is not angry and does not punish. According to human nature it is natural to get upset when we see actions labeled as "evil" and thereby to get angry at sin. But when we start to punish other people in the name of God, in our anger we have to stop and ask: who is doing the punishing? And does God really endorse this punishment?

If we take matters into our own hands and do the punishing on behalf of God, we better be very sure that this is what God wants us to do. I asked the NDErs about the statement: "Punishment is needed on earth to serve God's justice," and found that 64 percent said that they disagreed. One third, 36 percent, did express doubt through answering "not sure," but as with God not being angry we do have the same pattern though less strong.

This leads us naturally to the question: what is sin? I wanted to look at this question as well in my study and put the question to the NDErs taking part. To the statement: "Sin is conscious rebellion against God," only 28 percent said that they were in agreement and 50 percent said they disagreed. When I then asked if "sin is evil" I got an even lower rate of agreement of only 15 percent, while 54 percent said that they disagreed or strongly disagreed.

It seems pretty logical to conclude that if God is not angry and the Light is non-judgmental, then this evidence must also point towards the fact that the Light does not see "sin" in the same way we humans tend to do.

Edward tells us about his experience that,

For me the idea that I had been a sinner, or that I had sinned, weighed very heavy on my heart until my Near Death Experience. I really felt totally accepted – forgiven – and experienced a sense of compassion when my creator said to me: "I only want you to know that you are loved and accepted as you are.

Cheryl continues to answer this question by explaining that, "Sin is missing the mark. It's not quite doing it right and then you have a chance again to do it again until you get it right." This interpretation of sin as missing the mark is also what we find in ancient Greek thinking. Here next to missing the mark, *sin* means to "go wrong" or "fail to do."

The kind of failing here is connected to going wrong by losing one's sight, and this blindness of the truth brings us to an understanding of sin as false consciousness. If we see sin as false consciousness, it is also easy to see why punishment would not fit the crime. Punishment for something we do not understand and inflicting pain on someone who is lost and already in pain, is not a loving or compassionate action.

In the anger that causes us to fight against "evil," it is very easy to let our emotions run away with us and conclude that sin is always enlightened conscious rebellion against God. But in this connection, Danish philosopher Kierkegaard reminds us that Adam was innocent, when he was accused of the Original Sin. Yes, he broke the word of God, but Adam was still innocent because he was not enlightened as God, and thus, he did not understand the full meaning of God's commandment.

While Adam did hear the words of God, he was unable to fully comprehend the meaning of these words and comply with God's command because of a subconscious psychological event. Due to Adam's fear of the unknown, he was like a child who had to learn from his own experience. That the fruit was forbidden made the fear in him push his free will to overcome the fear by escaping his ignorance through the desire to know.

This subconscious attraction of the shadow is a well known aspect of human nature. Most parents know that forbidding something to their teen-agers without an in-depth explanation will create a backlash.

Underage drinking is a good example. Many parents also know that they cannot prevent their teen-agers from making the same mistakes that they have made, but that often children have to learn for themselves and by their own mistakes.

It is very hard to force our truth onto others with full respect for their individuality, and when you punish people for something they do not understand you get a reaction. Also there is a reason that we no longer hit our children in our efforts to teach them.

Now, while it may be easy to interpret the evidence from NDEs in line with Jesus as the Prince of Peace, it is more complicated when we have to fully comprehend the truth of what Jesus is saying or the testimonies from the Light.

Going back to our initial question about how God can be unconscious in the face of cruelty and abuse, and if we look beneath it, we can see that the question is really: how can God allow cruelty and abuse? This is one of the toughest questions of religion: How can God allow pain and suffering? How could God allow Saddam and Hitler to gain power?

However, there is a danger in asking these questions and going too deep within the sorrow without a foundation of love. The pain of the sorrow can lead to despair through the question: Why did this happen? Or how could God allow this to happen? This despair can lead to anger through a sense of powerlessness, and this anger can then again lead to doing another wrong. But as we all know: two wrongs do not make a right.

The anger and urge to seek justice through punishment is a natural human response to sorrow and despair. But, there is no evidence that this human emotion is the same way that God feels about it, and that we have the right to take God's judgment into our own hands.

In fact, what we can learn from the NDE is that the purpose of the life-review, or "hell," is not to punish but to make us aware. And as we just went through, these real experiences of God's forgiveness fits with the Greek understanding of sin as false consciousness or ignorance.

If we condense all sin, including the 7 deadly sins in Christianity, we end up with one sin only: false consciousness. This is the core or rather the reason that we 'sin.' From this and NDE research we can conclude that God wants to make us aware of the wrong, but we have no evidence to support that God also wants us to do wrong.

By going deeper within the sorrow on a foundation of love, we can also find compassion and understanding that makes us aware of the other. Thereby, there are two paths from within the sorrow: One towards despair and anger, and another towards compassion and learning from the sorrow. The first path leads towards more conflict and suffering, where the other path leads to growth and learning.

While hard to bear and sometimes understand, from a spiritual point of view sorrow can be seen as a gift because it forces us to seek God through compassion and understanding. Sorrow can be a progressive feeling that can wake us up from our pleasant lives and reconnect us with the Light of God, and as such, it serves as a positive spiritual force.

The meaningless of sorrow can also push us to look for meaning through growth and a deeper understanding. If we take the extreme case of Hitler again, a deeper truth can be found through the understanding that the horrible acts committed cannot be seen entirely as black and white.

First, it is reasonable to suggest that God is not responsible for everything that happens in this dimension, since we do have free will and some things are beyond our control. Also as we went through in the last chapter; we should be careful when we paint the world black and white in our search for purity that we do not end up in extremism.

The idea of Hitler as pure evil arriving out of nowhere in a world of pure goodness is taken out of context. While the time of Hitler was a devastating moment in history, it is an illusion to think that the world was all pure and perfect before he came along. Anti-Semitism was part of many cultures and social Darwinism was irresistible to a colonial mindset that was the international norm.

After almost 2000 years of condemning Jews for killing Jesus and the widely accepted 'science' of Eugenics that wanted to improve human genetic qualities at the time, it is not difficult to see how an extreme interpretation of Darwin's "survival of the fittest" could be perverted into Hitler's final solution. Also we should not forget that slavery had only been abolished about one hundred years earlier, and that in the U.S. racism was supported by law even after Hitler. It took 20 years and a strong civil rights movement for African-Americans to gain equal rights through the Civil Rights Act in 1964.

The winners of the war were themselves far from pure and perfect nations as the United Kingdom had a long history of colonial suppression behind it and the U.S. had acted in the same colonial manner through the so-called "Banana Wars" in Central America and the Caribbean. To understand Hitler's rise to power one must understand the history of Europe with the struggle for colonial dominance and the competition in nation building. Here among many reasons, WW1 is directly tied to WW2 through the Treaty of Versailles and the damages Germany had to pay.

History does not excuse these horrific actions but it makes us understand how these events where possible. Understanding this helps us put things in the right context and should get us beyond a strict demonization, where we paint what we argue against extreme black in order to make ourselves look extreme white and pure. This form of argumentation is in itself extreme as it's an attempt to force our distorted point of view onto reality through fear.

Secondly, I think that it is reasonable to conclude that we should also be humble towards the possibility that maybe here on earth we do not know all there is to know about God`s plan. This is another thing we can learn from the NDE as this testimony reveals:

When I looked into my soul and saw that I was pure love, there were a few seconds when I felt that I was looking out on all the world, understanding it and seeing that it was perfect. And seeing as it were through God's eyes I understood why it was perfect. Now, you come back down to this dimension it is much harder to understand. But I know that it is true God is all love.

Here Jayne reveals that in the Light she was able to understand everything. This is also a general finding in NDE research, where most people have a sense of perfect understanding as if all the knowledge of the universe and all its secrets are revealed to them in one moment.

In my study, I found that 66 percent would describe this moment as "Absolute perfection" and that almost nine out of ten, 87 percent, would describe this sensation as "Understanding." However, as Jayne also tells us, when the NDEr comes back from the other side into this dimension the perfect understanding of everything is lost.

This is very clear from NDE research as NDErs will say that the true nature and full understanding of their experience is beyond human comprehension. Russ' testimony here explains this paradox in a good way: "During the death event, I felt I had access to unlimited information but I couldn't bring it all back in raw form. Now, five years later, I am still deciphering it all."

The paradox that we are dealing with becomes more clear when we try to ask NDErs what exactly God is. Here 93 percent said that "God is a form of energy," and when we add to this conclusion that we are talking about an otherworldly dimension that in its full comprehension is beyond human understanding, then it forces us to be open to the mystery.

God's true nature and full mystery is beyond our understanding. Not that we cannot conclude that God is love and not angry, but the full and complete insight into God's plan or how to interpret God's will is beyond us.

From NDE research, we can clearly conclude that there is an element of mystery to the experience of God, and that the full knowledge of God gained in the Light cannot be comprehended here on earth in the body. Therefore, as with religion, reasonable doubt and humility should be part of our path towards God.

This openness and humility is often forgotten when we let human emotions, such as fear and anger, interpret the will of God. We may not be responsible for unintended consequences, but if our actions are based on arrogance and self-righteousness, we are responsible for this arrogance and self-righteousness.

The way out of this fundamentalism is to loosen our minds grip on extreme purity. This is what Douglas was talking about before when she said that a strict pattern of purity leads us into contradiction. It is only natural and also vital for our mind to be able to discriminate, but too much discrimination can lead us into extremes.

In the East we often find religions that use meditation in order to clam the mind with the aim of abandoning duality. E.g. Buddhism teaches that we must let go of the "poison of contradiction" within our mind because it leads us into extremes.

Extremism is neither peaceful nor holy because of its inherent contradiction that leads us into conflict. And as we have just seen the foundation of religion is to seek peace, and not conflict, so one should be aware of this danger of extremism not to be let astray into conflict.

Douglas explains about extremism: "That which is negated is not thereby removed. The rest of life, which does not tidily fit the accepted categories, is still there and demands attention...As life is in the body it cannot be rejected outright."

One could say that from a political standpoint, without using God as an alibi, a response to 9/11 was necessary. However, it is now clear that the aggressive attempt to negate terrorism through the "war on terror" and a preemptive war against Iraq has been an over-reaction that has had a heavy cost in lives. The injustice of a pre-emptive war has increased the level of terrorism including making it spread to other countries.

Through the negation of terrorism, it has grown in size and strength, and it has not been removed through the negation because the underlying causes of terrorism have not been addressed. As with most military conflicts, now even in Afghanistan the US has arrived at the conclusion that the conflict cannot be solved militarily and as part of the exit strategy there is now talk of a political solution involving the enemy.

The negation of terrorism is a good example of Douglas' argument and if we as Christians believe in the divinity of Christ we must at least attribute the same level of insight to Jesus that Douglas has. Politically one could certainly make the argument that something had to be done to prevent terrorism, but from a religious point of view there is no evidence that God wants us to actively fight terrorism in 'his' name.

Jesus did not seek to negate the Roman Empire through violence as he was concerned with helping the weak and sick. Does this mean that as Christians, or religious people, we can only engage in charity and humanitarian relief? Or does it mean that humanitarian intervention in Darfur is justified, while pre-emptive war against Iraq is not?

That I will not try to answer on behalf of the Light, or God, but surely these are questions we need to think about as a more enlightened balance with less extremism is needed in our search to do the right action in the name of God. Even if we insist that God acts through us there is no way we can defend unenlightened actions in the name of God.

If we go back to Douglas' argument again she is not only pointing out that what you negate receives power through your negation, as if you push someone they will usually push you back. She is also pointing out something more important and general: that we cannot reject the body.

Religion dealing in divine or absolute truth has a tendency to focus on the soul or mind through the rejection of the body. The body is where we find impurity or relative truth that is more down to earth than the inspiration sought from above.

No matter how devoted we are in our search for God, as life is in the body we cannot outright reject the body. And no matter how much we long to be united with God, we still have to live here on earth in the body. Since we cannot reject the body completely we are forced to accept the body, and as such, we will also have to accept earthly or relative truths.

Rather than rejecting the negation, as with the body, we may sometimes have to accept the earthly truths and seek peace through striking the right balance. We could call this the balance between the soul and the body, or the balance between the divine and earthly truth – the balance between absolute and relative truth.

As the abandonment of contradiction can lead us away from extremes, we also find that acceptance and tolerance becomes important in our search for balance. If we go back to the testimonies from the Light we can find something interesting. I asked David about what lesson he learned from his life-review and this was his answer:

Acceptance was a big lesson for me and with that life-review and those interactions I saw acceptance of other people as well. Before my Near Death Experience I was pretty brash, I didn't have much understanding of other people's point of view and I was very self-centered. If you didn't believe what I believed you weren't much part of my life. But in the life-review I got to see that there are other people's paths that don't have anything to do with me and that they can live their life. Now I have a tolerance for their path that I didn't have before, because I saw that they have their path and they have their purpose in life. And it doesn't necessarily have to agree with my path and my purpose. I can be tolerant of that. And that was a big lesson for me as well. I suddenly could accept who I was and I could be tolerant of others.

Acceptance and tolerance are found at the heart of all religions through the Golden Rule, and in the NDE the life-review is called the "ultimate teaching tool," where people experience this rule directly. Religion tells us to love our neighbor as ourselves or that we should not do to another what we would not have them do to us. From the NDE we can learn that the depth of this rule goes far beyond a mind that is clouded by fear, anger, arrogance, self-righteousness, or any other simple human emotion.

No matter how much we want to help others or how sure we are of the truth, our starting point when dealing with other people still has to be that of acceptance. Even if we believe that people have a false view of themselves and we are convinced that we know their truth better than they do, the manner in which we approach them still has to be respectful to them as an equal human being.

Even if we are convinced that the way other people see themselves is wrong, the way that these people see themselves is still valid to them. And as such, through tolerance and acceptance we must begin by meeting them there from this position of mutual respect.

In the case of the Iraq war and the removal of Saddam, we cannot say that the end justifies the means because we are overlooking the right to live of the hundreds of thousands of civilians. Their right to live and our acceptance of this right is not a means to an end, it is an end in itself. As with finding the right balance between the body and the soul, with Saddam we have to balance his brutal dictatorship with the cost of his removal. And we have to balance the choice of going to war with other alternatives.

God does not have to be unconscious in the face of a brutal dictator, but God may very well not be angry enough to pay the price of the heavy loss of life that is the result of war. Creative destruction where the end justifies the means does not uphold the Golden Rule because this false consciousness does not respect the right of our neighbor to live.

The Golden Rule is true no matter if we use the fight against evil or the fight against an ideology to justify the killing of our neighbor. Having history on our side means nothing without the Golden Rule because what we are creating in the name of history, we are creating through destruction.

Freedom from brutality or Democracy may be valid ends but this does not mean that we can write off the Golden Rule and endorse a blank check for militarism. As humans we may have a history of creative destruction through a taste for militarism, but this history does not mean that God endorses the destruction we cause in the name of 'his' creation.

Also on a deeper level, when things are going well it is easy to judge others based on our own standard or world view, but to genuinely help someone else based on the Golden Rule it takes an enlightened perspective that fully respects the other and truly loves our neighbor.

As a lesson from David's life-review that taught him to accept others and be tolerant, he also reveals how the rule works when we interact with other people:

We are going to exchange paths, we are going to cross paths and interact. Many times I may not agree with their personal views or what they are doing in life or what they want to achieve in life, but that is alright...I also saw in my life-review that we can all experience something together – you and I can have a shared experience – but the truth of that experience to me is going to be different than the truth of that experience for you.

This is a basic human insight into the Golden Rule and if we look deeper into this, we can see how truth can be different or relatively true. Both in religion and philosophy of religion we find that there are two directions: ascension and descension. Some people are ascending towards God in their search for God, but others having found God may be descending to earth in order do the work of God.

This means that some people look up to God in their search for God, while other people who have found God look down to earth in trying to find out how to do God's work. These are opposite directions and if we ask which direction, or which truth, is the true one we will arrive at the answer: None of them – they are both true.

This way of seeing truth as direction is another path to acceptance and tolerance. The truth of each individual is describing their choice of direction. A person who is ascending towards absolute truth will conflict with the truth of a person who is descending towards relative truth and from this perspective the conflict in not about truth but about direction.

In this conflict we should consider that our souls may not all be in need of the same lessons or fulfilling the same purpose, and as such some people, or souls, may need ascension while others may need to descend.

We should consider that maybe each soul has a unique journey and that there may be no competition in getting to the goal first. Also different souls may have different goals as they may have different paths. And if one of us has found a path, there may be other paths and our path may not be the right one for everyone.

Chapter Seven:

Hell as a Gift

Having just shed light on that God is not angry and what sin is, it is now possible for us to look deeper into what hell is based on NDE research and real experiences. First, however, I would like to establish the fact that negative or distressing Near Death Experiences do occur, and within NDE research there is also evidence of so-called "hellish experiences." Also just to put the record straight: just because NDE research concludes that God is not angry it does not follow that there are no consequences for our actions as people do have painful experiences.

A Gallup Poll in 1982 estimated that out of eight million NDEs in the U.S., only about 1 percent had an "unpleasant" experience. Some NDE researchers have come up with the same number of about 1 percent but they have also openly admitted an emphasis on pleasant or heaven-like experiences.

Researchers who have looked at unpleasant and hellish experiences within the NDE have found about 15 percent. Researcher Margot Grey found a high rate of 12 percent "hellish experiences" and Peter Fenwick found that 15 percent of the people in his study had "moments of terror."

Most reliable according to statistical certainty would be P. M. H. Atwater's large sample of 3,000 NDEs. She found that out of 3,000 adult NDEs 15 percent had "unpleasant experiences" and one third, 5 percent, had a hellish experience where they described it as "truly hellish." She also confirmed this number from a smaller sample of 700 NDEs where she found 105 cases of unpleasant experiences, which again makes it 15 percent.

Is there proof of hell then? We could conclude that hell is real based on these statistics and the fact that people do have unpleasant "hellish experiences" in their NDE. However, in an ultimate sense the reality of hell is complex.

In her article *Is There a Hell*, Atwater concludes the following:

Is there a hell? To one who thinks he or she has been there, the answer is yes. To a person like myself, who has studied what evidence exists and has conducted countless interviews, the answer is this: there is more to the near-death experience than anyone currently knows. The phenomenon is vast in scope, its implications more important and more dynamic than most people are willing to admit. Heaven and hell may seem more conceptual than fact, but right now they are all we have to go on as we search further afield into what the mind and its mental imagery might reveal about the source of our being.

The fact that people do have unpleasant NDEs with hellish experiences, does count as a proof that people do have experiences of hell. However, as Atwater also tells us; hell may ultimately be more a conceptual reality or a state of being than an actual reality or literal place.

NDE research in general agrees with this conclusion that we cannot take these "hellish experiences" as an absolute proof of the dogmatic religious interpretation of hell. Naturally, when people describe leaving their bodies and going to a non-physical dimension we are not talking about hell as a literal physical place. Also as we saw in the last two chapters, the angry judgmental God of dogmatic religion does not exist in the light of NDEs. To confirm that God is not angry in relation to hell, I also asked about the following statement in my study: "God wants to punish us in hell." Here in total rejection 100 percent said that they disagreed with 86 percent saying that they strongly disagreed.

Then how are we to understand unpleasant NDEs in relation to the religious understanding of hell? This, as Atwater points out, takes a deeper investigation because the phenomenon of the NDE is vast in scope and has more important implications than most of us are willing to admit or accept.

The first fact is that NDE research finds a wide difference in the content of NDEs based on cultural differences. These differences are most evident in pleasant or heaven-like experiences where meetings with religious figures are clearly defined by the religious background of each individual. However, while we do find unpleasant or hell-like experiences in most or all cultures, there is still a difference in the cultural content of these negative experiences.

If we look at a couple of Western experiences of hell we can see how the content fits with a classical Western view of hell. The first person explains that, "I felt I was in Hell. There was a big pit with vapour coming out and there were arms and hands coming out trying to grab me."

Also in Fenwick's book *The Truth in the Light*, another person gives this longer testimony:

> *It was really like all the images I had ever had of Hell. I was being barbecued. I was wrapped in tinfoil, basted and roasted. Occassionally I was basted by devils sticking their basting syringe with great needles into my flesh and injecting my flesh with the red-hot fat. I was also rolled from side to side with the long forks that the devils used to make sure that I was being well and truly roasted.*

In both testimonies of hell we have the classical content of a Western hell and while the first person tells us she felt she was in hell the last person even explains that it was like all the images he had ever had of hell.

If we look at non-Western experiences of hell we will quickly see that the content is different. Todd Murphy published a study of Buddhist NDEs in 1999 where he looked at 11 Thai cases. While there was a higher frequency of distressing elements in these NDEs, it is very clear that they have specific cultural content as in ten cases people met Yama, the Buddhist Lord of Death or his servants that are called Yamatoots.

One account reveals that, "Yamatoot told him that he had to be judged. He then found himself in front of Yama, the lord of the underworld." Another person explains that,

> I looked and saw that they were Yamatoots. One of them spoke to me saying "we've come to take you to hell". I said "I'm not going", and I tried to escape. I turned and repeated that I was not going to go to the house of Yama.

Secondly, besides specific cultural content we also find that fact and perception can be very different. Not only cultural conditioning, but also the perception of each individual can play a major factor in how the NDE is experienced. Atwater explains that, "Invariably an attack of some kind would take place in hellish scenarios or a shunning, and pain would be felt or surges of anxiety and fear." But; "Amazing as it may seem, I noticed that the same scene that one individual considers wonderfully positive another may declare negative or horrific."

There is evidence to suggest that not only cultural concepts of hell play a factor in the perception of hell, but also one's environment may play a factor. First, the finding of higher rates of unpleasant NDEs among people with distressing states of mind at the moment of death, such as e.g. suicide attempts, seems to suggest that our mental state has an impact on the negative content of the NDE. Also higher frequencies of negative experiences have been found in other cultures, such as in African cultures where a belief in woodoo and a sense of being "bewitched" was predominant.

Also very interestingly, a German study that compared East German NDEs with West German NDEs happening before the fall of the wall, found a huge difference in distressing experiences. Where the East German NDEs had a frequency of negative experiences of 60 percent, the West German study only found 29 percent.

So, we find that not only is there is difference in cultural content but there also seems to be a difference in perception of what is experienced as distressing, and that both mental state and environments may affect the negative experience.

What does hell look like then? According to research of Near Death Experiences and accounts by people who have actually been there, that depends on what cultural conditioning you bring with you into death and project into the experience. And how painful the experience of hell will be depends on how intensely your projection is inverted.

Researchers Kenneth Ring and Margot Grey have suggested that the hellish NDE is simply a more intense version of an "inverted" NDE. This is supported by other researchers who conclude that the mind of each individual interacts with the Light and that each NDEr projects their cultural concepts and mental state into the Light.

If we go back to David's testimony again from two chapters back, we can find that he gives us a hint in this direction:

In my life-review, I experienced a lot of things that I was judging – me – the humanness that came along with me that I hadn't quite shed yet. Because I think dying is a process and I think that when we re-integrate into that light, it takes a while to distill some of our attitudes and leave them behind.

He explains that the "humanness" that he brought along with him was something that he had to let go of to re-integrate into the light. If we translate this "humanness" into the cultural conditioning and mental state that we bring with us, this testimony makes a lot of sense in relation to the conclusion of NDE research.

In her book *Return from Death*, Margot Grey explains that, "The hell-like experience is defined as being one which includes all the elements comprehended in the negative phase, only more so in that feelings are encountered with a far greater intensity."

In a painful experience of the NDE where a person experiences fear, anger, horror, isolation, or guilt, this person may become more negatively inverted, and thus, experience the unpleasant elements of the NDE with greater intensity.

Relating to this intensity of the experience, NDE research generally identifies three types of the unpleasant or negative experience. These types can also be seen as levels of intensity of the negative or distressing experience within the NDE.

The first level has all the common elements of a pleasant experience, only these are experienced as frightening. This is the inverted experience mentioned before. At the second level this inverted experience continues and all sense of meaning disappears where the person feels a sense of void. At the final level, people have hellish experiences that include hellish imagery, demonic beings and personal torment.

Level one and two are very similar to pleasant experiences, only the response seems to be that of fear or abandonment rather than a positive state of mind. However, when we get to the last level where we are talking about a hell-like experience with hellish imagery there is some evidence to suggest that these could be illusionary.

In an interview with Dr. Peter Fenwick, he concluded for me that by looking at the number of hell-like experiences he has had in his research, "It's quite clear to see that they are illusionary and that they fall very much into the category of the paranoid psychosis of intensive care."

One of the cases where this was very clear in Fenwick's research was one of the first testimonies of 'hell' we looked at before. Here the person explained that he was being "barbecued" and "basted by devils sticking their basting syringe with great needles" into him, and that he was "rolled from side to side with the long forks that the devils used" to make sure he was being well roasted.

This person had a very natural explanation for his experience of hell and tells us that, "Hell has an easy explanation – I was wrapped in a tinfoil blanket, an electric heat cage was put over me and during that time I was turned several times and innumerable injections were given."

Fenwick explains about this kind of experience of 'hell' that:

At that level one was dealing with not a straight forward near death experience, one was dealing with a sort of semi-confusional state that you see in intensive care psychosis. Is there a relationship between the mental state of the individual, or psychological state of the individual, and the near death experience? The answer to that is that there has to be. I can't see any objection to arguing that some people because of their personality structure or because of the various situations they are in, that there shouldn't be a wash-over of that into the experience, which is interpreted by them as negative. I think this is reasonable.

In my research into this area, I found that to the statement: "The visual images I saw were projections," only 40 percent disagreed and 50 percent said that they were "not sure." Also to the statement: "The visual images interacted with my mind," I found that seven out of ten, 70 percent, agreed with having a sense of interaction between their mind and what they saw.

This fits with the conclusion in NDE research mentioned before, that people who are in a distressing state of mind at the time of their experience of near death, such as NDEs caused by suicide attempts, have a higher frequency of distressing experiences. People who have been raised to expect distress at the moment of death may also be more prone to have a negative experience during their NDE.

However, while we do find that people's state of mind affects their experience and examples of people projecting illusionary content into their negative experience, there is still another element of the negative or hellish experience that does make sense. This is the involuntary event of examining one's past through the life-review, where people go through episodes of their lives and this part of the unpleasant or hellish experience is real.

Atwater explains about the final level that hell-like experiences often contain forms of "hauntings from one's own past," and that these are usually experienced by people who have deeply suppressed fear or guilt, and even by people who expect punishment after death.

Other researchers have concluded that the hellish experiences are "unfinished business," and if we relate the suppressed fear and guilt to a form of haunting from the past, then we can start to make some sense out of the hell-like experience.

If we conclude that the hellish experience is a more inverted and fearful perception of the life-review, then we can begin to make some sense of the experience of hell in the NDE.

It was an experience thrown upon me in the situation of near drowning. Not something I asked for, and the events that took place; the flashback of my life with commentary from some other being, followed by a light I was just starting to enter, were all involuntary experiences. I was simply along for the ride, but it was 100% real to me.

What Chris S. here tells us is that the life-review is both involuntary and 100 percent real. Life-reviews can be both negative and/or positive in content and they happen to about 30 percent of people who have NDEs. While NDE researchers tend not to support the dogmatic interpretation of hellish experiences, almost all accept the reality of the life-review as a standard element of the NDE.

The life-review is considered a basic element on most researchers' NDE scale, which is used to analyze the NDE, and thereby most researchers take the review as a factual element of the NDE. Kenneth Ring calls the life-review the "ultimate teaching tool" and explains that it is a basic "principle of life" that leads us to conclude the existence of the Golden Rule.

Another researcher, Dr. Bruce Greyson, explains that the NDE is evidence that the Golden Rule is not a simple figure of speech that we are taught to obey, but that it's an "indisputable law of nature."

From over 30 years of research, Greyson concludes that:

The bulk of the evidence points towards that after you leave the body, the soul becomes much less individualized and starts to emerge with something larger then itself – that we are all potentially a part of; we are all part of the same thing, that we are all interconnected, that as Jesus said: "what you are doing to me, you are doing to yourself."

In relation to our concept of 'hell' the negative or distressing life-review can be very deep and extremely painful whereby the review takes on its convincing function as a teaching tool. This we can understand if we go back to my finding in the second chapter, where I asked each NDEr to compare the sensation in their NDE to the sensation of experience here in this dimension on earth.

The result was that 78 percent said that the sensation was stronger than here on earth, with 26 percent saying 50 – 100 times stronger than in this dimension, and 53 percent saying a thousand times stronger or beyond description. In the category of thousand times stronger or beyond, we had statements such as "beyond my ability to describe," or so powerful it "cannot be measured."

Now, if we take this power of the experience and add negative or distressing elements to it, then we can see how the life-review can be very painful. Due to the intensity of the experience alone, one can understand how the painful life-review can be equivalent to burning in a fire, if we speak metaphorically.

Therefore, if we add the fear or guilt of a person who becomes inverted when meeting this power, we can see how the "hell-like experience" can become extremely intense and scary through the projection of imagery.

Most of us know how that in darkness, e.g. when walking through a dark forest, we are able to project fear that is not real and this would be something similar to an inverted hellish experience where our fear or guilt interacts with our experience.

The life-review is not only intense because of the power of being in the other dimension, but also through its closeness and honesty as David here explains:

> I was able to not only experience my life in review but also everyone I ever had an interaction with. There were multiple interactions and exchanges with everyone in the review. There were exchanges of energy, also cellular and molecular exchanges with everyone I interacted with in this physical life. Even when we focus our thoughts on one another these exchanges occur.

Also Connie gives a testimony about how the Light knew everything about her: "It was a multi-colored brilliant swirling ball of Light that was thinking. It had consciousness. It knew me – everything about me."

In Peter Fenwick's research, we find another NDEr that explains exactly how everything is revealed and that there is no escaping the truth of one's actions:

> There was no denying the facts because they were all there, including my innermost thoughts, emotions and motives. I knew that my life was over and whatever came next would be a direct consequence of not only what I had done in my life, but what I had thought and what had been my true feeling at the time.

This testimony reveals the life-review as a "direct consequence" and it brings into conclusion the insight from the last two chapters that God is not angry in the NDE. Most people do not have the expected reward-punishment crisis that we would expect from a hell that is a punishment.

If we go back to my findings on this, we will remember that where 80 percent used the words "truth" and "enlightenment" about this process, only 13 percent said "judgment" and even less, 6 percent, said "blame" or "guilt." Besides experiencing the truth as enlightenment, I found that 60 percent said that the element of truth in the experience wanted to "teach" or "show me the way, and 73 percent said "teaching me with love and compassion."

This means that the life-review without punishment and judgment is more a discerning of our actions – a compassionate discrimination – to help us see the truth.

Raymond Moody agrees with this in his original book *Life After Life*, where he explains that the review is more a kind of Socratic questioning to "provoke reflection," with the intention "to help the person who is being asked to proceed along the path to the truth about himself."

This interpretation of the life-review fits with our definition of sin in the last chapter as getting lost and having false consciousness. If God is love then it would only be natural that 'he' would want to bring our false consciousness back towards the truth with love and compassion.

In relation to hell in the Bible, we find that the Hebrew word for hell is "Sheol" and if we look into the root of this word, we find that "Shaal" means "to ask" or "to inquire" about something. Also when we look at the English "Helan," we find that it comes from "Hel," the goddess of the underworld, Helheim, among the Norse gods. And when we translate Hel into Latin we find that it translates into "Celare." Celare again means "concealed" or "hidden" in English, which brings us back to the truth being hidden for us when we sin through having false consciousness.

Also in Greek afterlife we find the Greek god Hades, who is the god of the underworld, and if we translate Hades we find that similarly to hell as hidden it means "unseen."

All of these interpretations of hell fit perfectly with the actual events experienced in the life-review of the NDE. First, we start with the extremely powerful sensation beyond human comprehension of leaving the body and entering the other dimension. Then we add the dissolution of our false consciousness and the life-review in this intense power and we can see how this experience can be painful beyond description.

Through this we can now try to understand what hell is by going back into the life-review:

I became distressed when I was shown and re-experienced unsavory parts of my life in the life review. I was judging myself and ashamed that my soul family had to experience this in my life review with me...Then I became disoriented when I started to experience things in my life that I had no reference to. My soul family again came to my rescue with loving support that got me through it.

Here David tells us that he became distressed when he re-experienced some of the less positive parts of his life. While he was judging himself and became disoriented, he also experienced that in the light his soul family supported him with love and compassion.

Another experiencer, Jacqui, explains that the Light was: "Very strong but welcoming and not disturbing...well maybe a little bit but I found it extremely profound and felt peace, love, beauty, warmth, an amazing experience."

What this points us to is another conclusion from the NDE, which reveals that even those people who have negative or distressing elements in their experience, still see their NDE as positive on a whole.

In my study, I asked the NDErs about the following statement: "Would you say that your experience was positive on a whole?" Here all of the people who had "distressing elements" in their experience said "yes."

Melanie tells us that, "The goal was to bring me to awareness," and from Dave's testimony we can learn that:

If I had to choose between the terms 'truth' and 'information' I would pick information...But there was never a question of their being truth contained in the information presented to me.

We can now begin to see hell as the inquiry into our life through the discerning of our actions, and if we see sin as false consciousness together with truth as valuable, then we no longer need to see hell as punishment.

Rather than a punishment, NDE research points to the conclusion of hell being a consequence of our separation from the Light or God. While upsetting to Christians who read the Bible literally this conclusion is not far from the description that Pope John II made in 1999, describing hell as: "the state of those who freely and definitely separate themselves from God."

As such the evidence from NDEs is much more likely to support the idea of Purgatory, where our soul is purified before our entry into heaven through the inquiry of the life-review.

In the Bible we are told that the power of the Holy Spirit is the "Spirit of Truth." Truth here is a power that the New Testament describes as a "fire" and that St. John on the Cross once called: "The Living Flame of Love." From this perspective God's anger is not anger but the raw truth of the living flame of God's love.

Also in the Catholic tradition we find the concept of "temporal punishment," which can be understood as the removal of unhealthy attachment such as sin. However, the 'punishment' here is not a punishment as such, but it is the pain of removing the attachment to sin through the spiritual fire of God's love as raw truth.

This fits with Genesis where we are told that when God cast out Adam from paradise, he placed a "flaming sword" to block the entry. Also in Matthew when Jesus talks about truth, he says that he has not come to bring peace but "a sword." Clearly truth is painful as the word sword is used, but also in Genesis when God condemns women to greatly increased pains through childbearing, we find that this pain has a double meaning.

When someone has been discovered in lying, the truth cuts painfully as a sword but after the pain is gone the person has been set free. And in the same way through the intense pain of birth new life is created. It is this new life of the spirit that is born in the painful flame of God's love. This new life is not a punishment but a blessing. We cannot be reborn and reunited with God without letting go of our ignorance and the attachment to our separation from God.

While God out of love and respect for us has given us free will, God cannot prevent the painful consequences of dissolving our pride and ignorance in the fire of truth because we choose to hold on to it. And because we are attached to it, the pain is actually the pain of loss. The consequence of free will is that the pain of losing our pride or ignorance is just as painful as losing anything else we choose to be attached to.

That hell is a consequence and not a punishment makes sense because if God as the truth is important, then getting out of our false consciousness through the experience of the truth must be seen as something good. Getting to the truth must ultimately be seen as positive or even a gift:

I felt my life-review was a gift to me because I saw my entire life, and I got to see it through other people's perspectives, through that exchange. And I got to see it in such a way that I suddenly knew who I was and I could accept this is who I am...Before my near death experience I was pretty brash, I didn't have much understanding of other people's point of view, I was self-centered...but in the life-review I got to see that there are other people's paths and now I have a tolerance for their paths. And that was a big lesson.

Calling hell a gift as David did here may be a radical idea for some people but it is to make us see things in a different light. If the truth is love and God wants to bring us to him – this love – then it is the separation from God that we should be afraid of and not the re-integration or the reunion with God. Going through hell or the life-review is a cleaning process that reunites us with God, and therefore, this natural process should not be feared because it brings us back to God.

This was also what Jayne said in Chapter Five, where we could learn from her testimony that:

> There is no such thing as an angry God. The God force or power that I felt was totally forgiving of any so-called error. In my wildest dreams I cannot conceive of God being interested in punishing. God is interested in bringing us to 'him' – to love.

God is love and returning to love is not a punishment. This is the great insight from the NDE that the thought of fearing Gods anger or hell is false consciousness. While we can fear the disconnection from God or the sheer power of leaving the body and entering the Light, we should not look upon the reunion with God through fear. It is a gift to be reunited with God.

NDE Researcher, Dr. Barbara Rommer explains that even though people who have distressing NDEs have to struggle through the emotional aftermath of their experience, still they almost always eventually come to see their experience as a "blessing in disguise."

Even NDEr Dannion Brinckley, who as a soldier had killed people and had to experience the painful consequences of his actions in his life-review tells us that, "I had felt the pain and anguish of reflection, but from that I had gained the knowledge that I could use to correct my life."

This knowledge gained by which we can correct our lives is also something that Atwater confirms as she explains that, although it is a surprise, hellish experiences can indeed be a positive experience: "unpleasant or hell-like experiences really can be quite positive if individual experiencers are inspired to make significant changes in their lives because of them."

In my own study, I also found this positive perspective. When asking about the element of coming to the truth through a life-review, Mary objected to the use of the word "consequence." She said that, "We will experience Karma, a balance of energy; I do not see it as a 'consequence', which has a negative connotation."

Finally, Nancy E. Bush who has studied distressing NDEs for over twenty years arrives at the same conclusion. In her article, *Afterward: Making meaning after a frightening near-death experience*, Bush tells us that:

A psychospiritual descent into hell has been the experience of saints and sages throughout history, and it is an inevitable episode in the pervasive, mythic theme of the hero's journey. Those who insist on finding the gift, the blessing of their experiences have the potential ultimately to realize a greater maturity and wholeness.

Chapter Eight:

God Within

"I knew I am now part of everything, we are all linked together via the source of life."

What Melanie here tells us is another general conclusion from the Near Death Experience (NDE), which points towards that God is to be found within. People who have NDEs are more likely to shift from being outwardly close to God to being inwardly close to God.

People will testify that God is in every one of us; that "everything is part of God" and that everything in existence has an essence of God within.

David reveals that:

The core of the experience I had was LOVE and Interconnection. I believe the Light permeates throughout everything. All of our physical reality has a component and a connection to the Light. Our physical presence is a manifestation from the Light, giving us the perception of separateness...Everyone and everything has this connection to the light.

This was the same conclusion I found in my study, where 80 percent said that "God is within" and 87 percent said that they agreed with the statement: "God is in everything." Russ explains that, "I remained as my unique self but I knew there was also a connection with God." And from Mary's experience we can learn that she had feeling of "connectedness to all things" and that she was feeling "God in all things."

That God is in everything and that God is within is not foreign to the Christian religion. In the Bible, Ephesians 4:6; we find that God is "above all, though all, and in us all." We also find a question in 1 Corinthians 3:16 by Paul that guides us in this direction: "Do you not know that you are the temple of God and that the Spirit of God dwells in you?"

This point may be evident and natural to many of us, but the reason that this message from the NDE is important for organized religion, is that forgetting that God is within can lead to religious fundamentalism. In order to organize religion and grow their numbers, some religions command their followers to love God before their neighbor.

This naturally leads to fundamentalism because it is a command to love a specific God that is put above the command to love our neighbor, and thereby, the comment to love God is opposed to loving a neighbor that believes in another God.

However, if we listen to the evidence from people that have NDEs then we can get out of this conflict by understanding that loving God and obeying the Golden Rule are in fact one and the same. Since God is in everything; God is also in our neighbor, even if this person believes in 'another' God, and thus, by loving our neighbor we are also loving God.

So, if we put the love of God and the Golden Rule together, instead of putting the commandment to love one specific God first, then we will find that the two commandments are one and the same.

"Thou shalt love thy God with all your heart, mind and Soul and the second part is just as important: Thou shalt treat your neighbor as yourself." Chris R. here tells us that the second part; to love our neighbor is "just as important" and this is what we can learn from the NDE.

We find the Golden Rule expressed in all religions and while some religions express this rule as a positive statement; to love our neighbor, others express the rule as a negative statement where we should not do on to others what we would not have them do to us.

The reason this is so important is that we can learn from the NDE that the Golden Rule has a much deeper meaning than most people think of because of our interconnectedness with our neighbor.

Michael tells us that, "I saw people, people I knew in life, and people I had never met but knew anyway." His experience of feeling that he knew people he had never met comes from the sense of oneness that most NDErs experience. This is the ultimate oneness that Chris here testifies about: "It's almost beyond description but somehow we ARE all ONE."

I found that Chris' testimony had full support by the NDErs in my study, where 87 percent said that they agreed with the statement: "We are all parts of one whole."

After giving their answer, I asked each NDEr to explain this sense of oneness and Priscilla explained: "I feel that since my NDE, everything is connected. We are all related and there are no divisions, and I feel that is the same with plants, animals and the earth too."

Giving a longer answer, David said that,

While in the light I was connected to all those fragments [of light]. It was like having the knowing from all the souls that ever were and all the souls that ever will be. Yet there was an even greater consciousness, a collection of the All, into the One.

Connie takes the meaning of this oneness further by first explaining that, "It's Oneness, and yet being aware of your uniqueness, too." Then, she goes on to explain what the consequences of this interconnectedness with our neighbor means:

I feel this would definitely be the end to all wars – if we only could feel another's pain and sadness that way, we couldn't harm anyone else. I believe it's because we don't feel another's pain as they do, that we are then able to engage in war, etc.

This is where the NDE gives us insight into the full depth of the Golden Rule. To the statement; "What you are doing to another; you are doing to yourself" I found that 86 percent agreed, and taking this insight deeper I also asked about the statement: "There is no other; we are the other." Here 83 percent said that they agreed, and when I went even deeper through the Mayan quote "I am the other you" I found that 62 percent said that they agreed.

Through this insight about our interconnectedness, we now have the reason that people experience negative life-reviews in the NDE. As we saw in the last chapter, the life-review is the ultimate teaching tool that teaches us the indisputable law of the universe: that all is interconnected.

Also the fact that people often have life-reviews where they experience themselves on the receiving end of their own harmful actions is a testimony to the deeper meaning of "we are the other." The lesson we can learn from the life-review in the NDE is that the Golden Rule is not simply a figure of speech; it has a deeper meaning than most of us can comprehend through the profound oneness of "there is no other."

From this deep insight into the Golden Rule, I would now like to spend part of this chapter to look into religious fundamentalism. Even though we may claim that our end is compassion for the other, the means of fundamentalism, which seek to force our way on to others, ultimately leads to the condemning or killing of the other.

Combining both the negative and positive manner of stating the Golden Rule we end up with: we must love our neighbor so that we do not hurt them. In order words: if we hurt our neighbor; we do not love our neighbor. Whether we talk about the Crusades, the discovery of America or the recent war in Iraq, it is delusional to speak of the killing of the other as the deep love and respect for the other, which the Golden Rule demands.

The angry delusional mind of fundamentalism arrives through the conflict of how to interpret the will of God. It is very evident that God is hard to find, or to prove the existence of God, in this physical world since Gods domain is otherworldly.

Remembering that in my study I found that 93 percent said that "God is a form of energy," then this clearly supports that while God is in everything, the ultimate place of God is to be found in another non-physical dimension.

Many of us recognize truth when we hear it or when we receive its inspiration, but there is a problem when you write down truth because truth is something living and something that is often difficult to put into words.

This is also what we can learn from the NDE because even though people are convinced they experience the ultimate truth, when NDErs come back it is hard for them to put this truth into words. I found that 80 percent said that they were either not sure if, or did not think that their experience could be "interpreted precisely in human language."

Here Russ' testimony explained this paradox between experiencing the truth and interpreting the truth in a good way: "During the death event, I felt I had access to unlimited information but I couldn't bring it all back in raw form. Now, five years later, I am still deciphering it all."

In the Bible, Romans 11:33 we find the same:

Oh, the depth of the riches of the wisdom and of the knowledge of God! How incomprehensible are his judgments and how unsearchable his ways! For who has known the mind of the Lord, or who has been his counselor?

Based on this we should consider humility rather than stubborn self-righteousness, and while searching the truth always keep an option for doubt in the back of our mind.

In Merriam-Webster's Dictionary, *"fundamentalism"* is defined as a movement within Protestantism emphasizing the literally interpreted Bible as fundamental to Christian life and teaching. If we define fundamentalism as the literal interpretation of the Bible, then a recent Gallup poll suggests that about one-third, 31 percent, of the American adult population is composed of fundamentalists through the belief that the Bible is the actual word of God, to be taken literally word for word.

Taking the Bible literally word for word leads to extremism and we are even told in the Bible that Jesus did not speak literally but in parables. In Matthew 13:10-11 we are told that the disciples asked Jesus: "Why do you speak to them in parables?" And Jesus answered why he spoke to the people in parables: "To you it is given to know the mysteries of the kingdom of heaven, but to them it is not given."

It is very easy to see how the belief that God is the undisputed author of the Bible, or any other book, leads straight to fundamentalism because then no human can argue against its words. However, while we most certainly can find divine inspiration in the words of the Bible and other religious texts, it is very evident that all of these were written by man.

In Christianity the earliest Gospels were written well after the death of Jesus, about 30 – 40 years after, and the title of each gospel clearly tell us: "The Holy Gospel of Jesus Christ *according to*..."

From the title alone it is very clear that God or Jesus did not write these words in person as the gospels were interpreted and written by Jesus' followers. And the books of the Bible we know today were put together at the

Council of Nicene in 325 AD almost three hundred years after Jesus. Here any reasonable believer in Jesus should not overlook the history of Christianity, where it was the Roman Emperor Constantine who laid the foundations of the Roman Catholic Church based on his desire for a uniform Empire.

Eusebius of Caesarea recorded that in Constantine's Letter to the Churches about respecting the Council at Nicaea, Constantine said this:

Having had full proof, in the general prosperity of the empire, how great the favor of God has been towards us, I have judged that it ought to be the first object of my endeavors, that unity of faith, sincerity of love, and community of feeling in regard to the worship of Almighty God, might be preserved among the highly favored multitude who compose the Catholic Church...so that no room was left for further discussion or controversy in relation to the faith.

This could almost sound noble, but mixed with the politics of a ruthless Roman Empire it is clear from history that Jesus' Kingdom of God became one with the Kingdom of Rome. And when one contemplates the teachings of Jesus, it could be pondered whether this was truly what Jesus wanted – that Caesar took control of God.

From Christian fundamentalists I often hear that the Bible is the literal word of God with arguments like "because the Bible says so" or "Jesus himself said so." But the fact is that we don't know exactly what Jesus said him-self because all we have are testimonies from other people about what he said. All we have is hear-say and as such we should be careful with taking everything literally and also mindful about separating the message from the messenger.

When we look deeper into fundamentalism we can see that this way of thinking actually shares similarities with the mentality of a child. Due to our instinct of self-preservation, or ego, it is natural that human nature is not good at receiving criticism because we see ourselves as the center of our universe. But for a child this reality is very more intense as small children strongly identify with their environment.

In child psychology we find that very small children identify with their surrounding environment in the same manner that fundamentalists identify with their belief. If a child is playing with a toy within its environment and we removed it, we will find that the child starts crying. The reason for this is that the child identifies with the toy, and thus through its removal, the child feels its identity—its whole existence—is being removed as well.

This kind of immaturity comes through the lack of having a separate and independent identity from the toy. In the same way, religious fundamentalism comes from a spiritually immature attachment to a religious figure or teaching. Non-attachment—to be able to reach God and receive the spiritual transmission—without being attached to the messenger, requires a certain spiritual maturity.

In Buddhism there is a famous quote from the Buddha where he says: "My finger points towards the moon but do not think that my finger is the moon." So, it is with religious fundamentalists because they are attached to the finger instead of the moon; the messenger instead of the message. Religious figures point towards God but they themselves are not God, and prophets speak about the truth but they themselves are not the truth.

Besides being spiritually immature and childish, fundamentalism also goes deeper than just the seemingly innocent literal interpretation of the Bible or any other book. In Greek, "fundamental" relates not only to what is necessary but also to something that is supreme, and from this basis the meaning becomes something achieved "by force" through "having power" or "authority" over someone else. Fundamentalism expressed through language is a "word of force" that as an act becomes the "constraining" of someone else by "applying force" on that person through enforcing one's opinion.

Thus, a fundamental view gives one the perception of being justified through the belief that one has "authority" or is "entitled" to dominate because of having the lawful power of holding "the truth." The supreme aspect of *fundamental* makes the fundamentalist "lord or master" over the holder of the "wrong view," who becomes forced into subordination.

Where Christian fundamentalism begins with forcing other views into subordination, is through the position that Jesus was the only son of God, or even God himself. This, however, should be seen in the light that Jesus was not the only son of God even in his own time. In fact, during the time of Jesus there was competition of this title as the Roman Emperor, Augustus, used the divine title *"divi filius"* – Son of God.

Augustus' image was on all coins in the Empire and his title was not to be missed by anyone, so therefore, Jesus and his followers were well aware of this. Based on this historical fact it is obvious to see the need among Christians to brand Jesus as the "only" Son of God because he was competing with the Roman Emperor.

Also another evident thing about Christianity is that the Bible has many contractions within it and we also find disagreement between the Apostles. Even the people closest to Jesus, the Apostles who's interpretations of Jesus' words that some Christians today take literally, could themselves not agree on how to interpret early Christianity.

In Galatians we find an open conflict between Paul and Peter on the issue of circumcision and who can take part in their new religion. Galatians also show Paul's frustration over the "foolish Galatians" in his attempts to establish a religion in the name of Jesus. This is also something we find in John where we are told that we, the people, cannot "receive" or "recognize" the message of Jesus, and thus, we find a motive for forcing the belief of Christianity on people.

In this relation David tells us that,

After my experience I spent a lot of time looking for the spirituality in many faiths, and I saw where many of the dogmatic religions used fear in trying to teach us a morality. I think that may have been appropriate in an earlier time. I don't necessarily feel it is appropriate today...I have more of a problem with the fear that religion uses than the anger because I feel like they use fear to try to control us to believe a certain aspect.

This fear in Christianity is best expressed through the view that if we don't believe in or accept Jesus Christ we will go to hell. Of course, none of us would like to go to hell, and so, this argument puts the full force of the true face of fundamentalism on our shoulders.

We find the source of Christian belief in Jesus as the one and "only" Son of God comes from the Nicene Creed from 325 AD: "We believe in...one Lord Jesus Christ, the only begotten of the Father, that is begotten of the substance of the Father, God from God, light from light, true God from true God."

As we find disagreement between Paul and Peter in Galatians, we also find great conflict of beliefs in the history of Christianity. The religion that turned Jesus into Christ was born out of great turmoil and we find many different beliefs and interpretations within the church.

Today after discovering the Gnostic Scriptures, the Dead Sea Scrolls, and other so-called lost books of the Bible we know that there were many different views and even Gospels in early Christianity.

In about 170 AD, Irenaeus, a church leader in France condemned these other Gospels in this way: "The heretics boast that they have many more gospels than there really are. But really they don't have any gospels that aren't full of blasphemy."

However, among these so-called "heretics" we also find great discontent for the other side as in the Gnostic Gospels, which call the God of the Bible "the jealous God" because this God said: "I am God, and there is no other."

At the center of this age old debate, we find the question of the incarnation which was fiercely disputed for more than a thousand years and is still alive and well today. After having conquered the entire Roman Empire in the name of Jesus, in 325 AD the emperor Constantine called for the council at Nicaea to settle what was called the Arian conflict.

Arius, a popular presbyter in the Alexandrian church, was condemned for his belief that the Trinity was a hierarchy from top to bottom: The Father, the Son, and the Holy Spirit. He firmly believed that while Jesus as the Son was great, he was not God incarnated.

Alexandria where Arius lived was at this time a melting pot of religious belief through the conquests of Alexander the Great, and many religious figures were translated into other religions as common ground for religious understanding was sought.

Much like today's global community, where many forms of fundamentalism are clashing, it is reasonable to suggest that Arius' saw the danger in the absolutism of interpreting Jesus as divine as it would be a source of conflict.

The Nicene Council voted against Arius and established the Nicene Creed that is still being read today where Jesus is the "only" son of God and divine as "God from God." However, the view of Arius that Jesus was not God had many supporters, and just 11 years later in 336 AD Constantine reversed the condemnation of Arius because he became convinced that this view was held by a majority.

Many bishops supported the view that the Son was not God, since the creator was believed to be unborn and uncreated whereby God could not become incarnated in absolute form. Thus, Arius' challenge: "Is Jesus unbegotten?" – Meaning that since God is un-manifest as absolute divinity and Jesus was a manifest man; the two are not the same.

This conclusion would be supported by NDE research because people tell us that their experience is beyond human comprehension, as the 80 percent that I found in agreement with their experience being difficult to describe or "interpreted precisely in human language." And if we look at the fact that most people say that they experience an unearthly realm or dimension that is non-physical, then we can see what Arius meant that Jesus is not un-manifest as God.

After almost 350 years of heated debate on this issue, in 680 AD, Emperor Constantine IV called the Third Council of Constantinople to establish that Jesus had two wills: one human and one divine.

This is the classical view of moderate Christians that we find today but because our western mind does not like duality, we have a tendency to mix the earthly with the divine. In this confusion of logic, no other event in the Christian religion shows us the danger in making Jesus God more evidently than the Crusades.

In 1095 at the Council of Piacenza the will of Christ, which began as the Lamb of God, had transformed into the support for the Crusades against the Muslims. Pope Urban II, who began the crusader movement in the name of Christ, is famous for saying that "God wills it" and that "Christ commands it." In Robert the Monk's account of Pope Urban's speech at the council, Urban is quoted as saying:

Let this then be your war-cry in combats, because this word is given to you by God. When an armed attack is made upon the enemy, let this one cry be raised by all the soldiers of God: It is the will of God! It is the will of God!

It is logical that when you incarnate God, rather than keeping the divine and human separate, you end up in a paradox where a God that says "Thou shall not kill" has changed his mind. Also without us being humble it is very easy for our own human fallible mind to get mixed up with the divine. Like the Crusades, the recent preemptive war against Iraq done out of "love of neighbor" shows the same ignorance and misinterpretation of a loving God.

Clearly when we look at the life of Jesus and how the Prince of Peace walked his talk, his will was taken to the extreme. But this extreme interpretation is the same dispute we find today when we accept the killing of others in the name of Christ and God.

Going back to our NDE research, with the agreement that God is within, I also found that 80 percent agreed with the statement: "God is within; we are God." Relating to Christianity again, we could say that if Jesus is the son of God then we are all sons and daughters of God. While Jesus unquestionably was a truly great inspirational figure, if he was God then we are all God.

Here the statement "we are God" is not meant as we humans are perfect as God, or as great as Jesus, but it is meant to focus on that if God is in everything then God is also a part of us – God is within. The important factor about this insight was as we saw in the beginning of this chapter that locating God within our neighbor makes us understand the Golden Rule at a deeper level.

However, the conclusion that God is within and that "we are God" also takes us into a very interesting part of what I found in this NDE research study. To the question: "Was the core or essence of your experience part of your identity; your true nature?" I found that 73 percent said yes.

Russ reveals that, "It seemed that I was the light because I felt what was happening to the light entity...I was the light. I knew that because I felt what it was obviously feeling." Also Michael tells us this in another manner where he explains that, "the Oneness was a very simple knowing that I belonged. It was just the knowledge that I was truly an aspect or facet of God, the Light, and All That Is."

Now, if God is within us and the Light is our true identity, then it would be very interesting to know exactly what this identity is within us. In my study, I got a clear hint of where to find our true identity through the statement: "Consciousness was at the center of my experience" where 86 percent agreed.

Of course, consciousness is how we perceive so this would be the logical answer, however, I also asked about the following statement: "The true nature of reality is pure consciousness." Here I found that 92 percent said that they agreed with the statement.

With also 92 percent saying that "what I experienced was non-physical" and 93 percent saying that "God is a form of energy," it is not far to concluding that God is part of our consciousness or the energy that makes up our awareness.

While this idea is most predominant in Eastern religions, it is not however, foreign to Christian religion. As we saw in the first chapter, in the Old Testament on Mount Sanai when Moses asks about God's name or who he is, "God said to Moses: I AM WHO AM." And in the footnote of verse 14 in the 1609 Douay Version of the Old Testament, we are told:

I am who am. That is, I am being itself, eternal, self-existent, independent, infinite; without beginning, end, or change; and the source of all other beings.

If we put this together with the Holy Spirit and conclude that the spirit within us is in fact our soul or pure consciousness then things start to make sense.

Greek for "spirit" is *breath* as in life, or the sign of life, and it is explained as "the life or spirit of man which survives after death." This connection is interesting when we know that in 4:24 John tells us that "God is spirit," which fits with

151

what Moses was told that God is being itself – the source of life.

What is really interesting about the Greek understanding of spirit is that one word used also means both "soul" and "mind." The same word used for spirit in Greek, *psyche*, means both mind and consciousness. This means that we can connect the testimony from the NDE that consciousness is the true nature of reality to the understanding of the Holy Spirit as both soul and mind or consciousness.

As John tells us that God is spirit, which can be understood as mind or consciousness, he also tells us where to find God in 14:17, "you shall know him, because he will dwell with you, and be in you." When we add all of this to the conclusion that God is within, then we are beginning to be able to make sense out of Luke 17:20-21,

Once, having been asked by the Pharisees when the kingdom of God would come, Jesus replied, "The kingdom of God does not come with your careful observation, not will people say, 'Here it is,' or 'There is it,' because the kingdom of God is within you.

Chapter Nine:

Heaven's Gate

In the research of near death experiences positive or pleasant experiences that contain an indescribable profound sensation of love, peace and joy are called pleasurable NDEs or "Heaven-Like Experiences."

P. M. H. Atwater found that out of her large sample of over 3,000 cases 47 percent of adult NDEs had a heaven-like experience. These experiences contain heaven-like scenarios where people are reunited with deceased family members, meetings with religious figures or beings of light, and pleasant life-reviews where positive episodes of people's lives are reviewed.

While each heaven-like experience is unique still we find an event that is very common, which is the meeting with the Light;

I began to go upwards. I don't recall seeing anybody or anyone being with me but I just felt so peaceful and calm. I have never felt that good in my whole life and as I went up it was like light coming down. I could see light around me and as I went up the light was real bright; it was beautiful, there were different colors in the light...I never felt this peace before and I wanted it to go on.

Wanda's testimony tells us about the beauty of "the light" that is the center of the heaven-like experience. People who have NDEs often used the word "heaven" or "paradise" to relate to their experience, however, most commonly we find the term "the Light," as the heart of what people experience in their heaven-like experience.

In my study, I found that while 40 percent would agree to call this the experience of "heaven," a lager majority of 73 percent would prefer to call it "the Light." This figure is similar to what other researchers have found such as Peter Fenwick, who found 72 percent in his larger sample.

What this leads us into is a very important insight of the NDE. As we saw earlier that we cannot interpret the hellish NDE in a narrow way, we also find in NDE research that we cannot interpret heaven-like NDEs narrowly either.

The idea that a particular religion holds the only key to heaven, or that e.g. Jesus is the only way to heaven, is not supported by research of NDEs. You often hear from certain Christians that "Jesus himself said that he is the only way to heaven," which is what you can find in the Bible if you read John 14:6 literally. But real experiences of people who die and actually go to heaven through the heaven-like experience do not confirm this belief.

In fact, if Jesus was the only way then people in other cultures would also meet Jesus as a universal experience or they would all go straight to hell. But they do not. When we look at cross-cultural research of near death experiences we clearly find a huge cultural difference in the content of NDEs based on cultural conditioning.

One example is a study of eleven NDEs from Thailand published by Todd Murphey in 1999, where we find that it is the Lord Buddha and the Buddhist Lord of Death, Yama or his servant Yamatoot that people meet.

One testimony explains that,

Finally I came to a temple wall. The Yamatoot took me to a large gate where I saw a monk giving a sermon to a group of elderly men and women. I made the formal gesture of respect to the Monk, and as I did so, I realized that the truth and highest form of help was to be found in The Lord Buddha.

We here see many of the specific aspects of Buddhism integrated into the experience through the concepts of a temple wall, a Monk, and the Lord Buddha. These contents of the Thai NDE are very clearly specific to the Buddhist culture of Thailand.

Also if we look at how these Thai NDEs are experiencing heaven, we will find that the description of heaven is very different than what we find e.g. in the Bible:

155

The Yamatoot took me up 27 levels. I saw many beautiful things in heaven. There were lovely pavilions in heaven, where jewelry littered the ground. I could not see anyone there. The Yamatoot told me that the people in heaven were arupa [formless] beings, and thus, were invisible. I heard monks chanting the Pali recitation "Shina Bahnchorn" [The Buddha's Window] the whole time I was in heaven. I had never been ordained as a monk, and so, had never learned the "Shin Bahnchorn" during my life. Nevertheless, I heard it constantly as I walked among the heavenly homes of that paradise.

In this testimony we have the experience of the "heavenly homes" as Buddhists believe in multiple levels of heaven and not one heaven like in the Bible. Also if we look at aboriginal cultures we find a very different picture of the cultural content.

In one of the Native American NDEs made public, that of Black Elk, we find that after collapsing in his tipi he was raised up into the clouds and had the following vision:

The circular hoop, the four directions, and the center of the world on an axis stretching from Sky to Earth, numerous neighing, dancing horses, surrounded by lightning and thunder, filled the sky at each direction.

Here we have clearly defined cultural characteristics, such as the classic Native American Mandala, Earth and Sky, and even "dancing horses." Also in my own study, I had one person from a First Nation background and I found that this person would use "Spirits," or "Spirit world" instead of "God."

If we go back to the chapter about hell and remember that 70 percent agreed that the visual images that they saw "interacted" with their mind, then we can get closer to an understanding of how people project their conditioning into their experience of heaven. And also if we listen closely to the testimonies that e.g. contain meetings with Jesus, we can see how people integrate their pre-existing belief system into their experience.

In fact, we rarely hear of NDEs where it is Jesus himself who tells people that: "I am Jesus." Instead it is very often people themselves who make, or jump, to that conclusion: "Then a divine presence, which I knew was Jesus, put his hands on my shoulder." Here it is the meeting with a divine presence "I knew was Jesus" and not Jesus who said: I am Jesus.

Another person relates that, "At the top of the mountain was this bearded man that could only be Jesus." Here we have the anticipation that it "could only be Jesus," and in another account we can see that the person makes the conclusion based on going to church: "It was like the Lord

157

talking to me and I knew it was the Lord because I've been in church all my life."

So, from this evidence and especially when we look at the cross-cultural contents of NDEs we find that the content of the NDE is not universal but conditional to each individual culture. Therefore, there is no evidence what so ever to support a fundamentalist view that Jesus or anyone else is the only religious figure people meet.

The basic conclusion from NDE research is that each individual integrate their own pre-existing belief system based on their culture into their near death experience. There is no absolute religious figure that we will all meet and there is no exclusive heaven or any one path that is the "only way to heaven."

In my study I found that 92 percent said that, "No one has a patent on Salvation or Heaven" and all, 100 percent, said that they strongly disagreed with the statement: "You need to believe in a particular religion to go to Heaven."

In fact, weather you believe in a particular religion or no religion at all does not seem to determine if you can go to heaven. NDE research concludes that pleasurable and heaven-like NDEs happen equally to people of different spiritual beliefs and religious affiliations, and we also find atheists that have heaven-like experiences.

In this account, Chris S, who was an atheist before his NDE explains that,

Keeping in mind that I was an atheist going into this event [NDE], I found it fascinating, based on Christianity which claims only believers will be saved, that there was absolutely zero negative comments made to me by the voice describing my importance to others in my life, and no sense of negative judgment based on my earlier belief. In fact, the warmth and joy sensed while just starting to go to the light was so intense that it was with some hesitation that I decided to attempt to snap out of my altered state to become lucid and try to free myself to surface and continue my physical life.

We find in NDE research that not only are atheists allowed into heaven, but as no religion has a patent on salvation and getting into heaven, we also find that in many cases people do not meet any specific religious figure at all but a spiritual authority that is neutral.

Jayne explains that, "I did not think to myself; this must be Jesus...or Peter, or anybody. I just simply recognized that he was a spiritual authority and I could trust this person." This spiritually neutral authority is more often than not expressed as a "being of light" or simply a "being."

Another NDEr, Dannion Brinkley tells us that, "As the Being of Light came closer, these feelings of love intensified until they became almost too pleasurable to withstand."

In his book *The Truth in the Light*, Dr. Peter Fenwick explains that,

Although the 'being of light' always has a spiritual significance, it is only seldom that people describe seeing a particular religious figure such as Christ. Even those people whose Christian faith is strong don't always see Christ. Much more often there is a feeling of 'coming before one's maker': the being is felt as 'God' in a very broad sense.

To back up his statement, Fenwick found that while 72 percent in his study experienced the light as the predominant feature of their NDE, only 33 percent saw or were aware of religious figures.

Also to understand what "God in a very broad sense" means Fenwick explains that the most common experience of the "being of light" is to be understood in a manner that is spiritually neutral. He says: "Perhaps 'neutrally spiritual' is the nearest one can get to the feeling the being evokes."

I also tried to go deeper into this by providing alternative answers to what God is and found that 73 percent would say "the Light," 66 percent "the Light of God," 60 percent "the essence of existence" and 53 percent said "pure being."

Also in trying to figure out what heaven is we find that this should be understood in a very broad sense as a non-physical place as well.

I asked about the following statement: "Heaven is a physical place" and found that 69 percent said that they disagreed. Opposite when asking about the statement: "Heaven is an unearthly dimension of energy" I found that eight out of ten, 79 percent, agreed.

Fenwick explains that,

Although many of these visions of Paradise include strong well-formed, visual images, sometimes the imagery is much less pictorial, at times almost losing its form completely. And yet it still remains intensely emotional, and still gives this very strong impression of heightened awareness.

One interesting piece of evidence that Fenwick also found in his study was that while 38 percent in his study met someone they knew, one third of that, 13 percent in total met someone who was still alive.

This of course makes us wonder that if heaven is a place where deceased loved ones wait for us, then what are living people doing there?

Along with the conclusion that the light interacts with our mind and that we project the contents of our mind into our experience of heaven, we also find that it is a co-created experience with both personal and impersonal events that we project into the Light.

As the Light is seen as the core of the experience, Atwater explains about The Evergreen Study that, "the light seemed to be non-physical; and if anything, the 'worlds' had their origin in the light, and not vice versa."

This conclusion fits my own findings as just mentioned that heaven is an unearthly dimension of energy. So, what is heaven then? Or what is the core and heart of heaven?

What Fenwick just explained was that although people have various visions of paradise, still at the core of the experience of heaven we find the very intense emotional state of love, peace and joy. This he found with 88 percent of the people in his study.

Then he also explained that the state of heightened awareness was at the center. If we take the strong impression of heightened awareness out of Fenwick's conclusion here and add it to what we found in the last chapter; that God is within as pure consciousness, then we are getting close to the heart of the experience of heaven.

On one hand we have the intensely emotional positive sensations of love, peace and joy, but on the other hand behind the visual images in the visions of heaven we have consciousness at its center.

This conclusion fits with my research where 93 percent said that "God is a form of energy." It also fits with the 92 percent who both said that what they experienced was "non-physical" and that the true nature of reality is "pure consciousness."

Having arrived at this conclusion now leads us to the next obvious question: Is it easy or difficult to enter Heaven?

This is a big question and the answer may not be as simple as it sounds. But we can learn a lot about the gate of heaven from people who have NDEs:

It allowed my being to find a comfort for transiting into the light. I didn't go through a tunnel; the light appeared in a distance and I moved towards it. I don't know if I moved towards it or it moved towards me, but there was movement into the light. And it was the most natural thing in the world, most natural thing beyond this world. It didn't require any sort of ritual. I didn't have to jump through any sort of hoops or anything. I was just a matter of...I was ready to go towards that light and I moved towards that light.

Here David gives us a very valuable insight from his NDE; that entering the light, or heaven, is the most natural thing in the world and that is doesn't require any ritual.

Also Cheryl explains the same as David here:

From my own experience it wasn't difficult at all. It was a staged process and like I said I don't think that I have been a perfect little angel. And yet, in my dying it was kind of in stages: I mean I first saw my body from a distance, I viewed what was happening, my body was *being destroyed and I watched it from a ways away. And then I found myself in a place of beauty, of light; bright aqua blue beautiful light. It was a place of perfect harmony and bliss. And then I found myself in the bright light. It's not like I tried to go or I had to be judged to go. I was the white light; I was in the white light. There was no difficulty in going there at all. So for me it was perfectly easy.*

"Perfectly easy" would fit with the majority of people in my study where I found that 85 percent disagreed that "Entry into Heaven is difficult and only for a few." In fact, NDE research agrees that entry into heaven is a natural process that we do not need to expend effort for.

I asked P. M. H. Atwater, based on her research whether heaven as a goal was difficult to reach, and this was her answer:

A goal is something that you do, it's something you achieve. It's something that you exert effort for. But returning to God, returning to that love, that reality; that's not something you exert effort for: that happens. That's a natural thing. Easy or hard that depends on the individual but it's a natural thing. It's where we go.

Atwater's answer gives us one of the main insights about heaven's gate that we can learn from the NDE: Entry into

Heaven is a natural process for all of us but as an individual we can make it difficult.

This deep insight into the gate of heaven and that there are two sides to entering the Light is also what we can learn from more of David's testimony:

It was very natural to me. I drowned and it was a very violent death because it was in a storm and it was very violent. Before I went into the light I found myself in a darkness but the darkness was...I can see where it might be frightening for some people. But for me it wasn't, it was more of a curiosity to me and it was warm and welcoming. And the transition from the darkness to the light just seemed like to most natural process in the world for me.

Here David admits that while entry into the light was very natural to him, he can still see how this process may be frightening to some people. In another part of David's testimony from chapter seven he also revealed that in order to re-integrate with the Light we have to shed our "humanness" and it is the fear of shedding this human aspect that can be frightening to some people.

Atwater explains further about the entry into heaven that:

Easy or hard that depends on the individual but it's a natural thing. It's where we go. Some people struggle against it because they can't believe it. Some people don't want to go back to that light, they want to stay here. They have their own perception, or their own idea of what the world is and they don't want to leave it. Maybe they are afraid, or maybe they believe some kind of story about death and crossing over and where they might end up. And indeed maybe some of those fears, or stories, or hesitations are correct because some people don't end up in pleasant places. The hellish experience is not rare; many people have hellish experiences.

Here we have to go back to what we looked at in the chapter about hell, where we made the conclusion that God is not angry and does not punish. However, for the same reason that entry into heaven is not one sided we also find that our view on hell is split into different perspectives.

Atwater also told us that she had yet to hear of a single experiencer in the world who had met an angry God in their NDE. But, she also revealed that while there is nothing negative in the Light, still people can be overwhelmed by the power of the experience:

As far as the one great light, what you and I would call God; no. Nothing negative, nothing horrific, nothing frightening...I am going to have to hitch a little bit on the word "frightening" because sometimes that greater light is so piercing and raw and so powerful that it is frightening in the sense that it is awesome. It is so awesome that it is overwhelming. So, in that sense it can be a little scary or a little frightening; not because it is negative but because it is so big and so powerful. So, some people are intimidated by that or overpowered by that.

The light is all love and there is absolutely no anger in God. But as Atwater explains even though our welcoming is so profoundly positive, still some people can be overpowered and intimidated by this powerful experience.

Here again we have to go back to the sheer power of the NDE that we have looked at earlier in the book. In chapter two we found that 78 percent said that the sensation was stronger than here on earth, with 26 percent saying 50 – 100 times stronger than in this dimension, and 53 percent saying a thousand times stronger or beyond description.

In the last category of a thousand times stronger or beyond, here more than half of the NDErs participating used words such as "beyond my ability to describe," or it "cannot be measured." This is how we are to understand the frightening aspect of entering heaven; as powerful.

This light exploded and went out in all directions. I could see it and this light spread out in all directions... but at the same time it was layering back endlessly. I have no words to describe this but yet I had enough awareness to think that I was perceiving linear time as well as dimensions – that's what I believe the layers were. It was infinite and not only was it infinite but there was nothing else to this light but love. And you know there aren't any words. If I had been in flesh I think that I would just have disintegrated in the power of this love.

Kimberly explains her experience of the light as an explosion and that if she had been in the flesh she would have been disintegrated by the power of the love. This is very common in the NDE where people often use the word "explosion" of love, or even a "cosmic orgasm," to describe the sheer power of the light.

There is usually nothing here in this dimension that comes close to this experience, which is why people say that it is beyond their "ability to describe," but Kimberly actually does make one good analogy. Relating her experience of going to Niagara Falls with two friends and going behind the water falls she reveals that,

They took me to Niagara Falls and they took me behind the falls and I was back in my near death experience. There was something about that thundering power of that water and the energy of being behind the falls. And I invite anyone; if you want to know what it might be like to be with this kind of brilliance and perfection and energy – you can get behind Niagara Falls and just let it...It's a glimpse.

Personally, I have used the parallel of the pull of gravity in the free fall, but the analogy of a water fall that Kimberly here makes is very good in trying to explain the power of being in the Light. We have to imagine that once we leave the body and enter into the other dimension on the other side, then the power and intensity of this otherworldly dimension is beyond human comprehension.

So, while merging with the light and entering Heaven is a very natural process, still some people do become frightened or overwhelmed by the sheer power of this experience. However, it is not God that punishes us in 'hell;' it is our own inability to embrace the profound love of the Light that makes us reject God. Ultimately, since we have free will it is our own aversion towards the Light and the profound love of God that makes us cling to something else through fear, guilt, etc.

Along with the fact that NDE research concludes that going to heaven is a natural 'easy' process, I will also reveal another very interesting finding in NDE research. Some research studies have suggested that the distressing or hell-like NDE is actually an incomplete experience and that when an NDE runs its full course the experience will be resolved into the peaceful, euphoric, heaven-like experience. This means that as we have just seen, if the heaven-like experience is a natural process the longer we stay in it the more we will let go of the fear and negative mind states to eventually end up in the heaven-like experience.

This would suggest that heaven is where we all go eventually. But still we find distressing experiences and that some people will find this experience too overwhelming. So, insight into what happens and especially how to steer out of a negative experience is important. While this is a huge topic, the simple answer here in this book is to know yourself or find God within you.

The way to embrace the Light and the full power of God's love is to understand who or what God is now. In the previous chapter we learned from the NDE that God is in everything and therefore also to be found within us.

Along with understanding the Resurrection as a spiritual event through the fact that we leave our bodies, it is also important to realize exactly who we are. Together with the 80 percent that agreed with the statement: "God is within; we are God," I also found that 73 percent said that this essence was part of their identity as their "true nature."

Upon revealing this finding, I will just go back to Jayne's testimony about death that gives us a very important insight about heaven's gate:

I did think at that time that the most important part of the experience was learning that there is no death...It took a few decades before I realized that looking into my soul and seeing that I was love was equally as important...possibly even more so, I don't know...but equally as important as knowing that there was no death; was knowing what I was, who I was; who we all are.

This same insight can be found in most Eastern religions where the true nature of reality is the same as our true nature, or our soul. It is said that all the 84.000 teaching of the Buddha can be condensed into three words: recognized your essence.

But also in Western culture do we find this same emphasis on recognizing our essence. In ancient Greece at the time of the birth of Western civilization, the most holy place was the Oracle in Delhi. Upon this oracle was written: "Know Thyself." To know yourself – to answer the question: who am I? – was the highest form of wisdom.

By now a devout Christian with a view narrowed by fundamentalism may already have stopped reading, but in fact, this thinking is very similar to the trinity in Christianity. If we take the Holy Spirit to be our soul as our true nature then it all fits together: God is within and we are one with God through our spirit or soul.

Realizing and remembering this makes us ready and able to meet God without being frightened because we already know God through the connection to our true nature within. Thereby, there are no surprises or frightening elements because we will not reject the profound love of God as we know God already.

In line with testimonies from NDEs we can find in the Bible, Mark 3:28 that "all sins shall be forgiven to the sons of men, and the blasphemies wherewith they may blaspheme." Also Matthew tells us this in 12:31, where he says that, "Every kind of sin and blasphemy shall be forgiven to men."

This is exactly what research of NDEs reveals as true that there are in effect no sins in heaven and that God is not angry at us. However, as the sheer power of this love and our meeting with God can be frightening, the Bible also agrees that there is one kind of "blasphemy" that will not be forgiven.

Matthew tells us that, "Whoever speaks against the Holy Spirit, it will not be forgiven him, either in this world or in the world to come." And in Mark 3:29 we are told that, "Whoever blasphemes against the Holy Spirit never as forgiveness, but will be guilty of an everlasting sin. For they said, He has an unclean spirit."

Now, we have gone through the meaning of sin and learned from the NDE that the anger and punishment of dogmatic religion is not what people experience on the other side. However, this part in Christianity, which people call the "blasphemy test," does make sense in relation to NDE research if we understand this "blasphemy" as the rejection of our soul, or true nature; God within us.

In other words, blasphemy is ignorance of our own true nature being one with God. Not knowing our true nature as the soul and pure consciousness is the ignorance that keeps us separated from God, and as 'sin' this ignorance is what causes the painful experience of the negative experience, or 'hell.'

This leads us to another related insight that I found in my study; that as God is within – we also find that heaven is within us as well. Chris tells us that, "We are here already; we never left Heaven," and this insight reveals a profound message from the NDE: that heaven is right here, right now.

Edward gives us this testimony:

In my experience of going into the white light…I recall the question that came to my mind: how could this ever happen to me? And the response was: 'this is where we are always if we could only remember.' The truth of who we really are – is now, always has been and will always be one with God. It is only our limited abilities to understand, to perceive and to experience that connectedness that gives us the belief that we are not in heaven or that we can't earn our way back to heaven. Everyone will eventually let go of that doubt, fear or self-condemnation that gives us the illusion that we are not connected to God and that we can't get back to heaven.

Here we have the first insight that "the truth of who we really are" is one with God, but we also get the insight that we are already in heaven. Edward reveals that the reason heaven is not a goal or something we need to exert effort for is that we are already there. All we have to do is to remember or let go and remembering means that we are already in heaven, right here, right now.

Some religious traditions will teach that because life here on earth is painful all we have to do is hold on till we get to heaven. However, this anticipation of going to heaven can not only make us see this life as meaningless, but it can also lead us into fundamentalism as we reject earthly life as unclean because we only want a pure life in heaven.

These religious traditions often reveal themselves through the rejection of evolution and a belief in the End Times. The Rapture is a good example where people find life on earth so unclean that they wish to disappear from the face of the planet and leave up to 1.5 billion of the rest of us to death and destruction.

But that life on earth is 'evil' or meaningless is not what we can learn about heaven from the NDE. Many NDErs will agree that heaven is here, right now. One way to understand this is that life on earth has profound meaning, which I found reflected in my study as 93 percent rejected the statement: "Life on earth is meaningless."

This is also reflected by the fact that most NDErs return from the experience with a sense of purpose that is part of a bigger picture that only Gods know all about.

David explains he didn't want to return to earth but that,

> The Light came back and it just resonated. It was dripping with love and it said: "No, you must return; you have a purpose." And when it told me that I had a purpose: that word just really seemed to resonate through my being. You have a knowing beyond what we are capable of and so when I heard purpose, I understood. And when I understood I had no choice but to accept it...I understood that returning to life was of the greater purpose. I understood that there was a higher purpose...A lot of that purpose revealed itself later in life and is continuing to reveal itself.

Another way to understand that heaven is here on earth is that our ability to love one another is here right now. This is reflected in my study where I found that 87 percent agreed that "Our chance to love is here right now."

This statement makes sense because if God is love, and the Light needs to work through us, then if would make sense that part of our purpose is to love. With almost nine out of ten saying that our chance to love is here on earth right now, it gives more meaning to the words of Jesus upon the tomb of Mother Theresa: "Love one another as I have loved you."

In remembering that the love of God is greater than our hearts and what we can imagine here on earth, these words point in the direction of the profound love of the Light. This is also the reason that we find that 80 – 90 percent of people who have NDEs report positive life-changes, where they become more loving, compassionate, tolerant and helpful towards others.

Along with these authentic responses to the love of the Light, in Return from Death researcher Margot Grey tells us that,

> It would seem that, however the NDE is brought about, the prime purpose of returning to physical life is to gain an opportunity to try to live life in accordance with the knowledge obtained while on the threshold of death.

Also Bruce Greyson confirms that by telling us that the purpose of the NDE is "to change you, and to inspire you to change your world." With the Golden Rule being experienced as an indisputable law of the universe and the conclusion that we are here on earth to learn, this would seem to be the ultimate interpretation of the purpose of life according to the NDE.

As religion tries to create order out of chaos through directing human evolution towards God, the general conclusion from NDE research would be in full support of an evolution towards the Light based on the knowledge that God is love – truly profound love – beyond human comprehension.

Through the loving actions of Jesus, Mother Theresa and many other religious figures and saints, we are reminded of the words "all we have is what we give." And when we remember that the love of the Light is greater than our hearts, we can begin to see a whole new world dawn in front of us based on the Golden Rule and the commandment to: "love one another as I have loved you."

This then in conclusion would be the knowledge gained beyond death by people who have near death experiences, and it does indeed confirm the message found in all religions; that God is love and we must love our neighbor. But the NDE also adds that we must love our neighbor in order to love God because we all have God within us.

In the 15th century, Cardinal Nicolas of Cusa summed up this very same conclusion like this:

For within us God says to love Him, from whom we receive being, and to do nothing to another, except that which we wish done to us. Love is therefore, the fulfillment of the law of God and all laws are reduced to this.

Near death experiences are direct experiences of this deeper level of understanding of the Golden Rule. This deeper level of love for our neighbor is also found in the Bible, where as the NDE confirms God is far greater than our hearts and beyond our comprehension. Even though 1 John tells us that "no one has seen God," people who have near death experiences can confirm from direct experience that: "if we love one another, God lives in us" because "God is love."

And thereby:

Whoever lives in love lives in God, and God in him. In this way, love is made complete among us so that we will have confidence on the day of judgment, because in this world we are like him.

Resources

Find out more about Rene Jorgensen at:

www.ReneJorgensen.com

Stay connected with Rene Jorgensen at:

Facebook: Rene Jorgensen

Find out more about Rene Jorgensen's research at:

www.NDELight.org

Youtube: LightBehindGod, ReneJorgensenDotCom

Find out more about the International Association for Near Death Studies at:

www.iands.org

16750841R00097

Made in the USA
Lexington, KY
09 August 2012